Credit - Based Systems

as Vehicles for Change

Managing Innovation and Change in Universities and Colleges

Series Editor: Susan Weil

Introducing Change From the Top in Universities and Colleges, Edited by Susan Weil

Implementing Change From Within Universities and Colleges, Edited by Maria Slowey

Credit-Based Systems as Vehicles for Change in Universities and Colleges, by Robert Allen and Geoff Layer

Credit-Based Systems
as Vehicles for Change in Universities and Colleges

Robert Allen &
Geoff Layer

London • Philadelphia

This book is dedicated to Norbert Singer

First published in 1995

Kogan Page Limited
120 Pentonville Road
London N1 9JN

British Library Cataloguing in Publication Data

A CIP record for this book is available from the British Library.

ISBN (paperback) 0 7494 1244 5

Typeset by Saxon Graphics Ltd, Derby.
Printed and bound in Great Britain by Biddles Ltd, Guildford and King's Lynn.

Contents

Series Editor's Foreword

Credit-based systems in themselves are not new. They have been long taken for granted in the US. Not so in the UK until recently, when the pressures of a declining investment in higher education, and more diverse student bodies and expectations, have made them much at issue. What makes the UK different from the US is the extent to which such systems can stimulate and support major change in higher education institutions, and in the values, practices and mental models of academics and managers.

In order to look critically at these differences, I recently took a group of senior managers and professionals in further and higher education within the UK to the US to examine in depth the changes that were taking place in higher education institutions. Each of the five institutions we targeted for what we called 'learning raids' had something distinctive to offer, things that were of much relevance to the UK scene. For example, there was the opportunity to examine the experience of those who had long been involved in the accreditation of prior experiential learning and development of leading edge systems for outreach, learner support and guidance. Equally alluring were those renowned research-based universities where something that was still challenging the very foundation of UK education – credit-based systems – were completely taken for granted. As the large group made their preparations, prior to breaking into 'raiding teams', you could touch the excitement in the air: that thrill of going back to the source whence the leading edge of changes in the UK had been derived.

Over the first two days, three teams immersed themselves in the processes and issues of the first three of the five targeted institutions. They ferreted out experience and tested working hypotheses about change in relation to a whole variety of issues that they had identified as important to their own concerns within the UK. They entered into this in-depth action learning/research process with the advantage of having had access to information and often confidential papers prior to the 'institutional raid'. These had often given considerable insight into the intentions, policies, processes and practices of each institution.

By Wednesday, when we came together again to examine findings across the teams, something powerful had happened. It was perhaps best captured by the suggestion that we rename the programme: from 'Learning from America' to 'Learning with America'. The role of the American experience in the group's learning process had shifted from a centre- to an off-stage position. For we began to recognize how much further and deep the changes in the UK were reaching. Credit-based systems could be significant influences here – especially on taking for granted thinking about education, entry, the role of student experience, etc – in ways that would be little understood in a system, where the most elite and the most pedestrian institutions take mass higher education and credit-based systems for granted. Fifty years ago, in that particular context, perhaps it felt differently. But the raids gave participants the opportunity to look beyond the structures towards the issues that the introduction of those structures raised. There was as much to learn from the UK experience – and as the week wore on, the catalyst of the US experience continued to provide good grist for our mill, as we considered what *else* was important for credit-based systems to make a difference: style of introduction, management values, professional leadership, sophisticated understandings of learning processes, etc.

This is where this book comes in. David Robertson's leading-edge work, *Choosing to Change*, made a major contribution to the debate. This, however, does the same, but from a different and more grounded perspective. The authors have personally lived through the significance (and the perceived insignificance) of all of the major issues arising out of the introduction of credit-based systems. On the one hand, the book offers an analysis of this cultural change in the particular historical and cultural circumstances of the UK higher education sector. On the other, it illuminates organizational, management and professional dimensions of change, revealing the consequences when these fail to cohere with educational developments. As importantly, the authors explore fully the potential for new forms of partnership whereby a concern with learning – in its full developmental sense – is placed at the heart of the system.

This book will be of value to practitioners and 'change agents' who continue to work against the grain of 'research first, students second' and want to make greater sense of their experience and indeed feel more confident about going further with such initiatives. It should also help managers to understand why 'top down and top heavy' introductions of credit-based systems can fail. It will assist professionals who wish to understand better the possibilities, limitations and change issues relating to the successful introduction of credit-based systems, and the role they might play in their introduction and development. And educators – in the community, in work settings and in colleges and universities – will benefit from the opportunity to reflect on the purposes of all this – for after all, it is not the structure that matters, but what happens inside and across the 'boxes'.

And this brings me to my final point. Fortunately, the authors help us to remember that credit-based systems are only a means to an end. As we learned in America, the credit-driven society is not necessarily a learning society. The risks of such a trend are already in evidence here. Students that leap through one hoop after another, ticking off the credits, with little opportunity to integrate, reflect on and make sense of themselves and their learning across these different modules, are not being developed for a world that is complex and requires us to think in holistic and connected ways. The challenge is how to ensure that credit-based systems support a learning experience that not only develops specialist knowledge and expertise, but also a person – who will indeed need those structures to move flexibly in and out of learning throughout their lives.

Preface and Acknowledgements

This book initially was a response to a perceived need for an account of a significant change in higher education, namely the rapid development of institutional structures based around credit. While much was being done, little was being written, and it was felt that a comprehensive account of what was happening, seen through the eyes of individuals who were directly involved, was overdue. Commitments and circumstances delayed the production of the book. In particular, the instigation of a project commissioned by the Higher Education Quality Council, the Department for Education and the Employment Department (with which both authors were closely involved) delayed, and in some ways superseded, the original conception of the book. *Choosing to Change*, the report written by David Robertson that came out of that project, is undoubtedly the definitive guide to the history and development of credit and modularity. In scope, scale and insight it will become an important document not only on credit-based systems, but on the UK higher education system in general. In acknowledging this, the authors also wish to thank David Robertson for the personal and professional stimulation he has provided over the years.

Meanwhile, however, Susan Weil and Kogan Page had established a new series on Managing Innovation and Change in Universities and Colleges. We wish to thank Susan for seeing that credit was a valuable tool for understanding the management of change, for encouraging us to explore the issues in a more personal way than is conventional, and for supporting us through the process of writing. We would also like to thank the two commissioning editors, Helen Carley and Clare Andrews, for their patience and tact.

Both authors have innumerable debts of gratitude to individuals. The book has a good deal to say about the strong national network of individuals involved with, and committed to, the development of credit-based systems. A strong and startling feature of this network has been its ability, in times when competition became a keyword, to share experience. We wish to thank all of them and hope that within the book they will find sufficient acknowledgement of their struggles and successes.

Another theme of the book is the importance of support from the top within organizations for individuals who must introduce and manage change. The authors wish particularly to thank Norbert Singer and John Stoddart for knowing when and how to provide that support.

Finally, there are personal thanks to Ann Allen and Jan Smith.

Chapter 1

The Development of a Flexible Mass Higher Education System in the UK: A Challenge to Management

Robert Allen

INTRODUCTION

From an élite to a mass system

The radical changes that have taken place within the UK higher education sector over the last decade are now evident and well documented. A catalogue of statistics can show how a once élite sector is being transformed into a mass system which by the end of the millennium will deliver levels of education that, in numerical terms, stand up against world comparisons. In practice, such comparisons will still show major differences between the UK and elsewhere, at least in terms of the quality, scope and content of what is delivered. More significantly, however, there remains the suspicion that while student numbers may have grown, it is far from clear that there are in place the cultural and structural changes required of the sector if it is to cope with its new status and clientele. To the participants within the system this transformation looks neither planned nor coordinated, organized nor resourced. Throughout the 1990s, initiatives and innovations have been rife, but seemingly delivered in a random and *ad hoc* manner, with little explanation or understanding of purpose or pattern. If the UK higher education sector has developed the means to support its transformation, it appears more a matter of good luck than an informed and well-managed process of change. This would not be a matter of great surprise to many working in higher education, either in the UK or elsewhere in the world. Indeed, it would seem to be more remarkable that any consistent trends emerged at all, rather than that the system seems to have developed randomly.

During 1994, however, a number of reports emerged from a variety of sources, speculating on the future of higher education. If anything was striking about them, it was the extent to which there appeared to be an emergent consistency, not only in terms of the issues that required resolution, but also in terms of at least some of the solutions. This apparent consensus was nowhere greater than in the area which is the concern of this book, credit-based systems, taken here to mean the development of flexible academic structures based around the parallel but interrelated concepts of credit and modularity. It seemed almost *de rigueur* – whether the report was from the Confederation of British Industry (CBI), the Institute of Education, the Employment Department, the Committee of Vice-Chancellors and Principals (CVCP), or the Higher Education Quality Council (HEQC) – to suggest that one of the required tools for delivering mass higher education is Credit Accumulation and Transfer, more commonly known as CAT or CATS.

While this apparent consensus may have the look of rhetoric, unsupported by much substance, its very prevalence and prominence is viewed with pleasure, tinged with some caution and even suspicion, by those who have been involved in the field of 'credit' over the last decade. It is also something of a mystery, given that a decade ago, with one or two notable exceptions, 'CAT' had the status of, at best, a fringe cult, and, at worst, an underground movement.

Credit as a case study of the changing system

Credit is a good example of a phenomenon that appears to have crept up on the sector. While it is an idea that most individuals within higher education will have heard of, even if only in the context of the US system or the Open University, its emergence as something that might provide the basis for a range of activities including funding is one of the more surprising stories of the decade. It is the purpose of this book to consider how and why this happened; to determine the sources and mechanics of change that underpinned its emergence; and to see whether it is possible to draw out some general management issues which will allow us to see how higher education might attempt to cope with the transformation it is undergoing. Credit is therefore seen as a case study that might illuminate some of the complex forces external to and within institutions, which affect the ability of the various stakeholders to influence and manage change.

In doing so, the book seeks to complement two companion volumes within this series which look, through individual accounts, at change from both the top and the middle of institutions. It also acknowledges, but does not attempt to replicate, the work brought together within the HEQC's 1994 report *Choosing to Change* (the Robertson Report). Whatever the consequences of that report's conclusions, it will undoubtedly come to be seen as a major and comprehensive account of the development not only of credit, but of UK higher education. This volume seeks, from practitioners' viewpoints, to bring together many of the issues of these other books within one case study. It relies significantly on our personal experiences, not only within our own institutional contexts, but on our work at local, regional and national levels. As such the emphasis has been on how change has been taking place. While it will provide an adequate background to the developments currently under way in the UK, it is not a definitive account of credit, nor is it a textbook on the management of change. It seeks instead to show how credit has been a tool by which a variety of players within higher education have sought to influence, and cope with, the dramatic changes of the last 15 years. Each chapter deals with specific aspects of the subject of credit-based systems – models of credit, institutional structures, students and staff, quality and professional development – but uses these as a base for us to reflect on the problems and processes, successes and failures from a personal perspective.

Evolution or accident?

There are those who will see in the relatively speedy development of credit-based developments within the UK a clear history, with evidence of evolution and even planning. It can be portrayed as an elongated but ultimately inevitable process moving from initiatives in credit and modularity in the 60s and 70s to a virtually universal credit-based system by the end of the century. It can also be argued that this is the only possible route for a mass higher education system to develop given the flexibility required by students and institutions alike in such circumstances. Proponents would point to the development of the US system during this century as exemplifying the demands made on, and solutions provided by, institutions having to respond to high participation rates in higher education.

In contrast, many academic staff would, understandably, see some rather more organized and hidden agendas sponsored by institutional managers and political agencies. They might argue, with some legitimacy, that it cannot be a coincidence that the very thing that is claimed to be good for the student also turns out to be the preferred methodology of those who seek to reduce the unit of resource and squeeze student funding. As such, credit practitioners can be perceived by colleagues as either dupes or agents of government and management.

A third view might be, of course, that none of this was planned, intended, or inevitable, and that the emergent changes are a consequence of complex forces being managed at different levels within institutions, and subject to unpredictable external market and political forces. As such, credit would be seen as having emerged as a common tool for organizing the delivery of higher education, in much the same way as IBM or subsequently MicroSoft technologies came to be industry standards: not because they were inevitable or best, but because they won.

The trade-off: education vs resources

None of these scenarios is necessarily wrong, nor are they mutually exclusive. The portrayal of good and evil is not, as usual, very helpful. It is perfectly feasible that a movement devoted to, and able to deliver, a better framework for students, might also be a tool for those whose interests are resource rationalization. Indeed it might be argued that the only acceptable and practical solutions to the current problems of higher education are ones where there are clear advantages to all sides of this particular equation. For an acceptable solution to current problems, there needs to be some sort of trade-off whereby the move to less resources is managed through a set of tools that enhances certain aspects of the student learning process despite the constraints. As such the controversies circulating around the introduction of credit reflect a wider debate about the future of higher education.

Given that mass higher education is necessarily cheaper higher education (in so-called unit terms), the essential question is whether the student experience, and institutional support of that (both academic and administrative), can be reorganized in such a way that not only are standards maintained but there are educational benefits. The reduction in resources is the only given, and one that most now accept will not change dramatically according to Treasury, political, or funding council whim. The nature of the reorganization of the system required to meet this resource change is not a given. All that is certain is that it cannot be done by maintaining the educational status quo and delivering higher education in its time-honoured ways.

People and paper

While nationally there appears to be an emerging consensus, much of the activity of the past decade has taken place within individual institutions, though supported by a continuing proliferation of nationally and regionally based projects and reports. No discussion of the development of credit during this period seems to have started without a quotation (usually the same one, and sometimes inaccurate) from the Toyne Report of 1979. This report has often been portrayed as the starting point for the subsequent move within the UK to credit-based systems. Its significance probably lies, not with its content (few people seem to have read it) or its major consequence (the establishment of the Educational Counselling and Credit Transfer Information Service, ECCTIS), but in the way it highlighted credit for the first time as a potentially significant tool for the UK education system. Its significance also lay, less obviously, in the simple fact that it was there, and therefore quotable, by those who wished to promote credit; and also in the personality of its author, someone in the grand evangelical mode, who was later to have his own institution to practise on. As we shall see in a later chapter it was that institution, Liverpool John Moores University, which was for a short time in the late 1980s to provide the most radical view of the way forward for higher education, one in which credit-based systems could become a vehicle for transformational change. It was important, therefore, because of its rhetorical value, a feature of the change process that is sometimes much neglected. Much of the early work within the field of credit-based systems was centred around principles and values, as practitioners sought to establish the credibility and utility of the tool. As we shall see, it is evident that at the institutional level this essential component of managing change – explanation and debate – was often dangerously neglected.

There were a large number of other reports which contributed, sometimes more substantively, to the debate about and the development of credit. By the late 1980s few reports on the future of higher education failed to mention CAT in one way or another. During this period, various agencies were funding research and projects which led to a wide range of reports on the principles and practice of credit and modularity. These, in a somewhat fragmented and *ad hoc* way, were to provide the guide book for those entering these fields. The speed of change, however, was such that it was not until the production of the Robertson Report in 1994 that a definitive and exhaustive analysis was carried out. But this report itself reflected the emergence of an extensive network of players involving institutions (at different levels), a variety of agencies, and leading individuals.

Sponsoring agencies

Credit has been supported by various agencies who, with a variety of agendas, have sought to influence higher education to move along this path. The major initial impetus in the 1980s came from the now defunct Council for National Academic Awards (CNAA). The CNAA's role as the national body responsible for awarding degrees in the polytechnics had principally been as a provider of quality assurance, but had always included a developmental edge, attempting to encourage change. By establishing a CAT unit, proposing a national tariff, developing regulatory guidelines, and making a highly public commitment to credit, it provided some of the carrots and sticks to move institutions in the direction of CAT. Without it, and particularly its introduction of an acceptable national 'currency' for credit, it is undoubtedly the case that the subsequent changes would have been neither as effective, nor as speedy. An equally notable, and frequently (and unfairly) disliked, agent has been the Employment Department which has over the last few years funded a large number of projects directed at introducing credit, and has also sought to be sympathetic when other projects have incorporated credit into their repertoire. Over the last few years, funding councils have also looked closely at, and sometimes supported, credit-based developments. It is interesting to note that the Robertson Report itself managed to bring together in a unique collaboration the Employment Department, the DfE and the HEQC as sponsoring partners.

Credit, has, therefore, gained a profile through strong national support and the availability of discretionary funding sources, that may well go beyond its current, sometimes marginal, significance within institutional portfolios. Put crudely, it has been easier to get money to support credit developments than for many other initiatives. Consequently, more has been written about credit, more conferences and workshops have been offered, and more projects have been reported on than many other significant practitioner-based initiatives, for example in the field of teaching and learning. Thus, for example, the assessment of prior learning (APL), has received considerable support but remains (and is likely to continue to remain) fairly marginal in even the most committed institutions.

The social network

The nature and significance of the social networks that have surrounded the development of credit and modularity must not be underestimated. In its early stages, the promotion of credit was based around a fairly limited and somewhat esoteric group of individuals, representative of, though clearly not always representing, the component parts of the higher education sector. It was a network that had its major powerful gurus, some of whom have gone on to become Vice-chancellors. It had its practitioner networks based either within existing national educational organizations or specifically designed regional credit consortia. It acquired its own meeting places and watering holes as it acted as a travelling roadshow throughout this period. Like all pseudo-evangelical movements, it developed its own disputes and factions, its obscure jargon and theological debates. Principally, however, it served to produce a national debate and some national consensus which could then be taken back into institutions.

What was particularly attractive to many was that it gave space for individuals coming up through the system to take an active role and gain profile. Indeed, the early gurus, now constrained by the need to run their own institutions, seem to have actively supported, within and outside their own institutions, specific individuals to carry the message on. A new generation of apprentice gurus were utilized to take on the debates and spread the word. They did this through a proliferation of conferences, workshops, working groups and steering committees.

This was sometimes a heady atmosphere. It was tempting for individuals, particularly in the conference bar, to see themselves as some sort of revolutionary vanguard. Such pretensions were, however, likely to be punctured by the perception of many of their colleagues that they were in fact stormtroopers. But in one sense, this network provided the basis by which credit could become a national, rather than an institutional issue. Many of the individuals were responsible for the introduction of credit-based schemes, and they brought to the previously theoretical debate experience and expertise that allowed others to move forward without having to reinvent the wheel.

Part of the significance of such networks lies in the ability of individuals to use them to rehearse and resolve issues outside of a specific institutional context. More importantly, however, networks can grow and develop to incorporate and induct new players as they and their institutions consider coming on board. If they work well they are both fluid and focused. Their members are able to utilize existing structures, or develop new ones. If successful, they can act as a Trojan horse into the system. They always face the threat of becoming static and self-perpetuating, but equally can become significant enough that they turn into something else or wither away as their tasks are achieved. In the mid-1990s such a turning-point has probably been reached, as individuals, groups and organizations either seek to leave, having served their purpose or found new interests, or to redefine their role to respond to the new circumstances.

Any analysis of significant change at a national level within higher education would find similar, if less noisy, networks. The successful and imaginative development of the Enterprise in Higher Education initiative (EHE) would be a good example, as would the Access movement of the 1980s. Similar networks would, of course be easily recognized as the traditional vehicle for much disciplinary and research development. The use of such social networks in implementing change is probably an area of research that would bear much fruit.

What also should not be underestimated is the significance of individuals, and their personality and charisma. While these could not be the basis of change if the environment were not correct, they are crucial to the successful and widespread acceptance of ideas. In this the credit movement has perhaps been luckier than most.

Gurus and disciples

The guru/disciple model can be carried too far, but is stronger than is often realized. Those involved in the development of credit in particular have a strong sense of a practitioner-based and possibly practitioner-led 'movement'. This has been led by a group of committed individuals, supported originally by a now powerful group of gurus who, while undoubtedly increasingly influenced by resource demands as they moved into their positions of power, retained a strong sense of the educational value of credit-based systems. This group, which has functioned fairly well as a national network, conveys a strong sense of ideological and moral overtones, seeing itself as responsible for being the vehicle for major change within their institutions and the system generally.

They of course carry with them some of the problems of being gurus, as do the disciples that trek along behind them. Too often they can be perceived as sanctimonious, naïve, short-sighted or perverse. Too often what they see as self-evident is perceived by colleagues as self-seeking or self-congratulatory. In the early days of credit developments at least, theory necessarily dominated practice and assertion overwhelmed evidence. Even when examples of good practice began to emerge, they were often rejected because they were seen as inappropriate to a specific institution, or were perceived as being imposed from outside. It has been one of those areas where it has been very important that a sense of personal ownership of the development by those working within an institution has been a crucial basis for successful innovation. The crude importation of external wisdom on the subject can therefore be counter-productive.

The commitment of members of this group is often genuinely behind the student, and it is the use of some of the more marginal tools associated with credit (such as Assessment of Prior Learning [APL]), together with a much stronger sense of the need for students to devise their own programmes of study, that separates many credit practitioners from those whose agenda might be more managerially derived or circumscribed. However, even this can work against them because such strongly student-centred approaches are inextricably linked in the eyes of many academics to a reduction in their own power. As a result, the credit practitioners may well have to come to see themselves as evangelists, needing to 'convert' those around them. In doing this, they have needed to avoid the wish to become martyrs, though the reality has been that some have come dangerously close to achieving this status.

A personal account

One of the themes of the series of which this book is part, is the use of personal 'stories' so that change is described 'not as history recounted at a distance, but rather as living struggles with "grotesque turbulence" ' (Weil, 1994, p.14). While this is an ambitious project for any manager or academic, made more difficult by its very public nature, it is possible to look at my own particular story and those of colleagues and friends, and see the way in which the history described above is reflected in individual and institutional histories, and also see how our own stories have impacted in diverse ways on the panoramic historical account. In some small way, it is possible to mirror the grand story with the personal account.

As a social anthropologist returning to the UK at the beginning of the 1980s my interests and concerns were probably not different from those of many other academics. Indeed my principal interest was to continue my research, for which purpose I needed a job. Having spent much of the previous decade abroad, mass higher education, access and credit were not, it should be said, at the forefront of my mind. However, taking a job in a then inner-London polytechnic and working part-time for the Open University undoubtedly exposed me to new influences, as did having both a parent and a partner who had gone, or were going through, higher education as mature students. I also had not experienced the 'good old days' of UK academic life in the 1960s and 1970s about which I heard so much, and I therefore had very little to reminisce or get nostalgic about. Finally, and fortunately, I found myself working with, and for, a number of people to whom accessibility was seen as central to their own educational values. Many of these new influences were subsequently internalized through my work with Access students as well as a highly diverse undergraduate student body.

None of this necessarily made me anything other than an academic with a predilection for wanting higher education to be more accessible. As such, while I may have been evolving, it required a number of 'accidents' to force or allow me into the arena of credit and modularity.

University managers are well advised to enjoy committee work, and it was a presence as a representative on university committees, together with a role as a NATFHE branch official, that in my case provided the required accidents. The University, which was carrying out a major funded project on the use of credit to develop in-company training, had obtained a few thousand pounds of money to carry out research into how to use credit within a non-modular system. It was, it would appear, something that no one else wanted to do. On what basis I accepted it, I seem to have forgotten, for I was strongly advised by colleagues not to touch it. I knew little about credit, and did not have a great deal more interest. While flattery may have played a part, a liking for the euphemistic 'challenge', and a realization that the education system was undergoing change, might be more noble explanations of why I accepted. In this sense my own activities were no more considered, planned or focused than many institutions who were in the next few years to take on credit and modularity.

My first task was to find out how others had done it. At the time, there was very little choice. A few institutions were involved in credit-based projects and they were to be the focus of the developing market in workshops, as well as providing the venues for pilgrimages. My own project itself became a learning experience both for myself and my institution which during this period began to gear up for the development of a CAT scheme and, before long, the process of unitization and semesterization. Suddenly I moved from being the reluctant and inexperienced researcher and became the 'expert'; the project became the classroom; and the subsequent research report the bible. It was not long before, as with many other colleagues, I was to become the 'CAT person', and to find myself seconded into the centre of the institution.

The way both my institutional and my personal story were to develop is described in some detail in Chapter 3. Both owed much to the way the university was managed. The predominant mode was an elongated developmental approach to cultural and structural shift and this suited me. I was, however, dependant on strong support from the centre and particularly the Vice-chancellor and to the support of a small group of academic staff within the institution who, with considerable zeal, pursued and promoted the virtues of credit as a device for opening up opportunities for students. With this support, what started out as a marginal activity was soon to become the mainstream.

This situation was replicated for me outside the university where a general lack of knowledge and case-law made becoming an expert a relatively simple task for those who sought, as I soon did, such a role. For the enthusiastic or the ambitious, many opportunities were opened up. Credit and modularity had by the early 1990s become a 'boom' area. The positive response I and my colleagues received in the external world often compensated for the difficult change processes we frequently experienced within our home institutions.

This relationship between the internal and external worlds replicated the broader battles and debates as external agencies attempted to impact on the supposedly resistant world of higher education. The excitement for individuals such as myself came from mediating that relationship, filtering out some of the external excesses for the requirement of the internal market, and simultaneously establishing a position in relation to the demands of the external world which reminded it of the realities of academic institutional life. Talking to and arguing with colleagues with similar dilemmas in other institutions became a vehicle for determining tactics, calculating risk and finding solutions.

An interesting example which highlights some of the tensions experienced by individuals was the contrast between my apparent hostility to NCVQ in the public arena, and what appeared to be my simultaneous promotion of it within my own institution. This was neither contradictory, nor disingenuous. NCVQ was clearly going to be a major player in post-16 education, but required substantial alteration if it were ever to be acceptable to or successful within higher education. Universities were rightly cautious of the new organization and its views of the nature of education, but would ignore it at their peril. This dilemma needed to be represented and debated. Reworking and reframing of the internal and external worlds for each others' consumption is a crucial role for those involved in development.

My own involvement in the external world, my exposure to the gurus and their evangelical statements, and my contact with other similar practitioners were all central to providing the armoury for both myself and my institution to develop and promote credit. It provided textbook and manual. These national activities also permitted institutions, through their members, to influence, even if in small ways, the national developments. The sharing of experience outside of institutions, became part of the development of some limited national consensus.

MANAGEMENT OF CHANGE

Collegiality and managerialism

The discussion of the management of change within higher education is always distorted by a still persisting view that managerialism is an inappropriate device for directing the activities of educational institutions. While it is possible that much of this is either rhetoric or misdirected nostalgia, it is still a crucial factor when institutions attempt to make significant transformations. An abhorrence of managerialism can be an effective rallying point from which to resist change that disturbs and threatens. It has become a conventional nostrum within higher education to say that this is a different issue for the ex-polytechnics, where managerialism is supposed to have prevailed for two decades, as opposed to the traditional universities where collegiality is often stated to be paramount. As always the reality is more complex and, in any case, one only has to look at the considerable powers of the old university Registrar, and the inability of the old polytechnic Directors to cope with Deans, to realize that the contrast is more likely to lie in the different distribution of managerial (sometimes disguised as administrative) power, rather than in the existence or non-existence of such power. As Middlehurst (1993) has commented, many of the significant features of the management of old universities are 'now more symbolic than real'.

Management from the top

In the volume that launched this series, the editor Susan Weil spent some time considering the theoretical and practical significance of the concept of 'managing from the top' within universities and the eyebrows that this might raise. It is not difficult to find Vice-chancellors within old universities who prefer to present themselves plaintively as 'last amongst equals' rather than Chief Executives. Many managers within universities would themselves resist an overemphasis on the notion of 'the manager'. They are quite content to admit, as Adrian Webb, Vice-chancellor at the University of Glamorgan, did in his chapter 'Two Tales from a Reluctant Manager' (Weil, 1994, p.42) that they 'stumbled unintentionally into senior management'. Indeed my own history replicates that particular tale. However, one cannot imagine managers in other sectors than education, even were this true, admitting it, never mind publishing it. The cult of the expert amateur still finds a place within higher education, and the principle of academic-cum-manager is still highly valued, even within the supposedly managerial new universities. The view that managers are probably born, possibly nurtured, but preferably not trained, often holds sway. It is intriguing to watch the recently arrived head hunters assiduously seeking out candidates for Vice-chancellor posts who have a commercial or industrial background, and regularly emerging instead with a Deputy or Pro-Vice chancellor as the successful appointee.

One must beware of falling too easily for the reluctant Vice-chancellor syndrome, or, conversely, for the view that trained managers are the only way forward. Higher education will be no different from other sectors in having incompetent trained managers working alongside their brilliant but intuitive counterparts, or vice-versa. It remains the case, however, that educational institutions create a different challenge for managers, as does any organization whose so-called 'products' are based on the activities of highly trained, partly autonomous, professionals. However, this should not preclude a view that an understanding of organizational and change management theory would normally help rather than hinder the success of many managers.

The management of uncertainty

Much of this debate about the existence or non-existence of managers in higher education relates only, if at all, to a time when things remained relatively static. Nowhere within the sector has this been the case, however, since the early 1980s. Then, if anything, it was some of the old universities that, as a result of significant budgetary cutbacks, were expected to manage change (and particularly redundancy) in a way that must have looked much too close to the industrial management model for comfort. But the need for rapid expansion within severe resource constraints, together with increasingly high levels of external accountability, makes the emergence of hierarchical, managed, structures within universities and colleges now seem inevitable.

In a situation where the relationships between an organization and its external stakeholders are less predictable and more significant, and where the internal structures need to be flexible and responsive enough to cope with uncertainty and change, if not chaos, the nature of university management must be different. As Christopher Price points out:

> *much change is neither bottom up nor top down; it is driven by a range of near-invisible, and sometimes unacknowledged, external pressures – new technology, funding formulae, performance indicators, curricular fashions, student consumer whim, institutional competition and other governmental fads – the effects of which strike participants late in the day.* (1994, p.29)

In her valuable and comprehensive account of the notion of leadership within academic institutions, Robin Middlehurst looks carefully and clearly at the traditional model which emphasized individual autonomy, expertise and reputation; a dual hierarchy of professional and administrative authority; and the value placed on consensus, reasoned argument, self governance and self-determination. As such, institutions were held together by tacit values and norms, loose coordination and control mechanisms, adequate resources, and no competition for their professional monopoly of 'higher learning'. The last decade, however, has seen major changes as a result of the alterations to the external environment. As a consequence, universities have:

> *tightened their coordination and control systems (assisted by information technology); streamlined their decision making processes; integrated their academic, financial and physical planning; improved their cost-control procedures; devolved many managerial functions from institutional to basic unit and individual levels; restructured operational units; created new functions and posts (public relations, marketing, a development office); developed new policies; and shifted from collective to individual managerial responsibility and accountability.* (Middlehurst, 1993, p.189)

She acknowledges that these changes have created tensions that have led to conflict and fault lines within institutions, but also stresses that '(P)erceptions of change have by no means been universally negative' and indeed may have created a 'buzz of excitement' or 'positive energy'.

Models of management

One of the problems of the debate about managerialism in higher education is that it often makes certain assumptions about the nature of management that, among management theoreticians at any rate, have gone out of fashion. Ironically, some of the values of higher education, and particularly such concerns as the need for power to be devolved, have over the past decade been regarded by fashionable gurus as critical to the management of any organization. Flat management structures, lean top management, small teams, ownership by those who deliver, devolved autonomy and responsibility, are ideas (if not jargon) that should be attractive to many in academic life. Indeed their similarity to traditional notions of collegiality are, on the surface, striking. The managerialism that is so abhorred by many academics is one that is no longer seen as adequate to a situation where sensitive and speedy response to external environments and markets are required. Much of the rhetoric of gurus such as Rosabeth Moss Kanter (1983), Henry Mintzberg (1983), or even Tom Peters (1992), would, if given a chance, stand up in general terms to the filter of a collegial value system.

Seeing this as an opportunity to base university management on modern theories would, however, underestimate the ability of many within higher education to resist even that with which they might, in principle, agree. It would also risk neglecting the capacity of some higher education managers to throw out the baby with the bathwater by discarding elements of useful and proven (but possibly 'traditional') models based on higher education, and then either overplaying modern management theory, or aligning themselves with classic management models that play straight into the hands of their opponents. But, if the management (and the managers) of change are now inevitable in modern higher education, and there are available management models that at least attempt to promote approaches and values which bear some resemblance to those traditionally held within universities, then it is beholden on university managers to look carefully at their options. It is always a danger that the stumbling amateur looks first to known, and probably old, models of change management. The disdain shared by many higher education managers for management training, except at the basic skills level (time, information and resource management), exemplifies and exacerbates this.

It would be my view, however, that managers in higher education should be cautious about viewing either traditional notions of collegiality, or fashionable gurus (or a hybrid of them) as providing a simple answer to current management problems. Having flirted with 1980s change management theories, while simultaneously trying to introduce changes through credit-based activities, I had been caught up in the excitement of both, each of which had the attractions of being impassioned and evangelical. While an important source of motivation and support, it became clear after a number of years of actually engaging in operational change, that reality was more complex and less dramatic. My feelings were acutely summarized in a book by Eccles and Nohria (1992) – appropriately called *Beyond the Hype* – when, in pursuit of the 'contemporary excitement about the emergence of radically different approaches to management' (p.viii), they suddenly found themselves beginning 'to feel that the connection between this impassioned rhetoric and real, nitty-gritty organisational action was more complicated than we had been ready to concede' (p.ix). From that point on they began to 'discover that many apparently new age organisations had within them old and well-established practices; that many of the apparently new ideas were themselves reformulations of much older ideas'. They therefore began to look at what they now saw as the 'hysteria', 'frenzy' and 'hype' surrounding the modern organization. The result, they said, has been 'a dazzling array of what are often perceived as management fads – fads that frequently become discredited soon after they have been widely propagated'.

Such a view would not come as any great surprise to most academics or many higher education managers. Indeed, they would wonder how it had taken so long for the Emperor to be exposed. The value of their book, however, lay in what they did with that realization about the hype of much 1980s theory, and their subsequent conclusions have some significance for understanding the contemporary changes in higher education and indeed for this book. In brief they concluded that they needed to return to the 'three true elements of effective management: rhetoric, action and identity' (p.9). For them, managers live in a rhetorical universe where language is needed not only to communicate but to persuade and even create. Managers need to take action which accomplishes short-term objectives while preserving long-term flexibility. And finally, in order to take effective action, managers need to understand the unique identities of the people with whom they deal in highlighting the relationship between what we say, what we do, and how that impacts on our identity within an organization. Through these three concepts, they provide a useful set of hooks on which to hang the complex changes within the UK higher education system, and in particular, the way in which credit-based systems have been developed. How relevant their framework is to this area of action is summarized by their comment that:

> *much of the current management discourse lends itself to the frenzied adoption of designs. The appeal of these designs lies in their broad generality and in the fact that designs are generally much easier to put into words than processes or actions.... All the same it is important to point out that we are not hostile toward design when used effectively as a management tool.... What is harmful, however, is when designs are understood as an end in themself rather than as a means of encouraging and facilitating action.* (p.13)

While it is not the purpose of this book to pursue or test their ideas systematically, their themes of the relation of language to action and identity constantly crop up as central to the processes of introducing credit-based systems. Ultimately, their simple view that management is the effective use of language to get things done would be a useful slogan for anyone working in this field.

Conclusion

The 1980s and 1990s have seen massive transformational change within higher education. Much of what has happened inside institutions has been a reaction to external changes within the social, political and economic environment. While some have greeted these changes with a mixture of support and concern, the overwhelming reaction on the part of many staff will have been that much that they valued has been lost, and that their professional expertise and power has been diminished alongside the experience of the students they teach. However much they might support the development of increased and wider access, the costs will have been too great.

In dealing with these changes, and in attempting to redress some of the imbalances that have arisen as student numbers have dramatically increased, the unit of resource has declined, and student funding has been massively eroded, institutional managers have sought to find means by which they can reconstruct their institutions and the working lives of those staff and students who inhabit them. Credit and modularity, developed initially in easier times because they were thought to be beneficial to students by allowing more choice, have been perceived as tools that might resolve some of the issues, and allow institutions and students to regain some element of control over a system that threatened to overwhelm them. Potentially they are tools that can be used to manage the new circumstances in a way that could prove of benefit to a variety of stakeholders in a situation where the only clear certainty is that everyone will have less money. Higher education managers, in determining that this was the way forward and then operationalizing that view, have met considerable resistance to the tools. To many academic staff (as well as significant groups of administrators) they have not been seen as the salvation of the system. Quite the opposite, they have frequently been regarded as a part of, indeed a principal cause of, the perceived decline of higher education. Much of this disjuncture may, I would argue, be as much about the ability of higher education to manage change, as it is about the tools. In the subsequent chapters we will look at how this scenario is unfolding, assess the utility of credit and modularity as effective agents of change, and consider the various models by which change is implemented.

Chapter 2

An Introduction to Credit-Based Systems

Robert Allen

CREDIT AND MODULARITY

The relationship between credit and modularity is surrounded by a series of arguments and myths. For those who have been responsible for the introduction of either, a lack of understanding on the part of academic and administrative staff alike of what is meant by, or involved in, their development has presented major problems. A particular difficulty is the assumption of many staff that there is only one model and that it is borrowed directly from the US, or early UK initiatives such as Oxford Brookes University or the Open University. The subtleties and complexities of the various alternatives are rarely understood. Unfortunately, it would seem that they are rarely explained either. In this chapter, I will look at some of the historical and structural features of both credit and modularity that are needed to understand the options open to institutions. The ability to determine and debate a model appropriate to particular institutional circumstances remains a crucial feature of the process of implementation. As I have argued earlier, an understanding of the rhetoric underpinning credit and modularity is as important as the technical detail.

Part of the problem is a confusion over principles as opposed to structures. It is worth identifying the underlying principles of both credit and modularity, before looking at the range of institutional structural arrangements they can support. The difference is, in fact, a simple one.

Credit

Credit, which is in many cases referred to as CAT (Credit Accumulation and Transfer), works at the broadest level by suggesting that learning can take place anywhere; that any learning can be measured and given a credit value; that credits for learning can be moved from one place of learning to another; and that a tariff with a wide acceptability is required to act as a currency to ensure the maximum portability of credits. It makes no assumption that learning must take place in an educational institution, or that it need be formal. Nor does it make any assumptions about what 'size' learning should be. It simply says that learning can be measured, accumulated and transferred. The simplicity of this is often neglected, or overwhelmed by the technology of systems, structures and regulations.

As such, credit claims to take as the starting point the student, their previous experience, and their future personal and professional needs. It attempts to undermine a central assumption of much of the UK higher education system, namely that learning best takes place within one institution, over a fixed and limited period of time, according to rules best determined by academic staff. Using credit, however, the workplace, the domestic environment, and private providers can be incorporated into higher education provision and students may have the opportunity to move across the various boundaries. This is clearly a tool which, whatever its quantitative marginality, has a qualitative significance that goes, as we shall see, well beyond conventional models of modularity such as were introduced in the 1970s. The ability to give value to, and transfer, credit has opened up areas of higher education which would have been impossible over a decade ago. These are discussed in some detail in Chapters 4 and 6.

Modularity

Modularity, in its most general sense, is very different. It makes an assumption that *formal* learning, mostly within educational institutions, can be broken into self-contained blocks (*units* or *modules*) in which students can learn and then show, through assessment, that they have satisfactorily done so. These blocks, which may be related to each other (for example, through the use of *prerequisites*), can then be built up by the student into appropriate academic awards. The crucial point, however, is that the modules are self-contained in terms of outcomes and assessment. Importantly, the general principle does not make any assumptions about size of modules or the need for standardization, though it is often assumed to.

Modularity is often assumed to refer to the sort of highly centralized administrative arrangements that were introduced alongside the 1970s modular developments of organizations such as London Guildhall, Hertfordshire or Oxford Brookes Universities. As a consequence modularity (and sometimes as a result, credit) is inextricably linked, wrongly in some cases, with centralized, top-down, resource-oriented management. Whatever the truth of these views, the consequence has been that introducing modularity has come to be seen as an issue relating to a major change of the balance of power within an institution. In practice however, the modularization of the curriculum can take many forms with diverse structural and management requirements. For this reason, some institutions have chosen to describe the process of developing module-based programmes as unitization, leaving the administrative and management arrangements supporting this to be determined within the institutional context. These debates are dealt with in more detail in Chapter 3.

It is important that these distinctions between modularity and credit are clear when institutions seek to introduce either or both of them. Some of the problems faced by those who must introduce change come from the confusion between, and conflation of, the principles and the practice underlying the two concepts. For example, the general principle of credit is frequently equated with the specific set of regulatory arrangements, usually called CAT, which emerged from the work of the CNAA. While the obvious relationship between the CNAA's work and the general development of credit-based systems has been crucial, the distinction between the principle and the practice needs to be maintained. Credit, fortunately, can exist without the CNAA CAT scheme.

Additionally, it is important to understand that modularity and credit are being developed, evaluated and sometimes decried in relation to what is assumed, particularly in ex-CNAA institutions, to have been the norm of the UK higher education system, the integrated coherent single honours degree. The fact that this creature has itself often been mythical – with many old universities having had partial modular structures for many years – adds to the lack of clarity over the nature of modularity and CAT by overemphasizing the radical nature of the difference between the old and the new.

Modularity and credit clearly, therefore, have a number of things in common. They both suggest that learning can be built up from separate blocks that can be uniquely valued. As such, both are tools with the capacity for delivering learning in a more flexible way. They are similar in offering students the potential for some power and flexibility over how, when, and even where they learn. In these very important senses, therefore, they are complementary and compatible. In one equally important sense, however, they are different. Credit can go beyond the individual educational institution; beyond educational institutions generally; and even beyond *formal* educational provision. But both are just tools which can be used in different ways, jointly or separately, for different purposes.

It is useful, therefore, whatever their interrelatedness, to see the general principles of credit and modularity as quite separate. Modularity allows for the reorganization of both an institution's curriculum and its management structures. Credit allows learning to be measured wherever it takes place. This conceptual distinction is important because in practice modularity and credit get confused and conflated as institutions struggle to introduce and develop them.

These distinctions are significant because an important part of any implementation process should address the issue of why particular changes are being undertaken. Who are they for? What do they achieve? Why this particular change and not some other? What is the additional value coming out of the change that makes it worthwhile? Individuals involved in introducing change need to be able to grapple with the very real, legitimate concerns over the purpose and value of introducing what is often very radical, time-consuming change. It is almost certain that, in the introduction of either credit or modularity, this explanatory phase has been the most neglected within many institutions. University managers have often behaved exactly as their critics would claim, with a centralized imposition of the changes which has failed to consult and debate with, or involve in other ways, those who ultimately deliver the system. Credit evangelists themselves have often borne some of the blame, ignoring the fact that in 'empowering' the student, they must first empower the staff.

Semesters

Confusion about modularity and credit has been exacerbated by the development within many institutions of the semester-based academic year. Many of the problems faced by those introducing credit or modularity are as much to do with the often simultaneous process of semesterization. The educational arguments for semesters are fairly strong. Semesters allow more choice for students than year-long modules, and necessitate less assessment for both staff and students than term-based (trimester) modules. However, for many academics, the semester is in their view simply too short to provide a genuine educational experience. This academic debate might be resolved were it not for the administrative nightmare that has emerged as a result of imposing two semesters on what is still in most UK universities a three-term academic year. The problems of providing end-of-semester assessment just after students return from a Christmas vacation, and the mechanics of then marking essays and making decisions in a one or two week inter-semester break, have exasperated even the most ardent modular practitioner, and frustrated the most effective administrator. It can work, but I have long ago given up pretending it is other than a 'pig's ear' model.

For a number of years there has been a very strong demand from all levels of institutions to introduce what is usually known as the Stirling model. The University of Stirling has from its earliest days had a semester before Christmas and a semester after the extended vacation. While this is somewhat easier in Scotland, where the problems caused by late A-level results do not prevent an early September start for the academic year, it should not be beyond the higher education sector generally to deliver something similar. There has indeed been considerable momentum from many institutions, but concerns about the back-door introduction of a third semester, and a reluctance on the part of most institutions to go it alone have delayed a concerted effort to solve the problem. In 1994 a small number of institutions broke ranks and it remains to be seen whether this will become something that the majority of institutions will take on board. In the meantime, however, the management of an inherently flawed semester structure creates a range of problems that frequently undermines the successful implementation of modularity and credit, and can create a set of barriers to the acceptance of credit-based systems by both staff and students.

CAT

An example of this lack of explanation is the very term CAT itself, which in this book we have sought not to use except in particular contexts. As an acronym, however, it has been widely used. Robertson seeks in his report to have it excluded because, he argues, it engenders confusion. If people are asked what it means, a range of opinions emerges. To some, particularly in the old universities, it relates to little more than the 120 credit/year tariff, introduced by the CNAA and now adopted, if only in principle, by a majority of institutions. However, in such situations it may have an added and more significant meaning in that it is perceived as an alternative, and inherently less desirable, way of doing things. In its potential, it can come to symbolize threat and disorder.

To others it can have a much more positive meaning. For them it is a term that relates to a certain type of student, namely one who has the opportunity to design a customized package constructed from across an institution's curriculum, possibly having brought credit from another source through the assessment of prior learning (APL). It has also been used, particularly in the late 1980s, to identify a specific structural formation within an institution. Thus, institutions wishing to develop the model of CAT students introduced CAT units and CAT coordinators. These individiduals and units may have had broader roles, including the development of modularity, but their principal role and structural position was on the edge of mainstream provision, with a remit to deliver this alternative approach for a limited number of students. Over time it may have been the intention (frequently unstated) to turn this alternative into the mainstream, but initially CAT as a phenomenon took on a marginal position within many institutions.

As a consequence, the term CAT never provided sufficient consensus to bring together the underlying flexibility and the diverse forms of practice that might emerge. The subsequent preference of many (including myself) for 'credit' or 'credit-based systems' as generic terms, is an attempt to pursue principle without making too many assumptions about specific practice.

The importance of these issues of terminology and language have been underestimated in discussions about the implementation of change. Higher education managers, as perhaps with managers in any other sector, have often neglected this aspect of change. The arrival in institutions, often unannounced, of terms such as CAT, modularity and APL, without sufficient support and explanation, makes resistance almost inevitable. It is a new language describing apparently new and unproven concepts. Ironically, some of the activities – for example APL or even modularity – have been carried out for many years under other banners without necessarily upsetting people. The need for people to understand and eventually own the language they are expected to use is critical.

Credit-based systems as a tool for change

If we can disentangle the various different though interrelated activities that sometimes lurk under the banners of credit and modularity, they can, separately or in combination, provide a powerful tool to direct and manage change. The significance of their simultaneous and interrelated development over the past decade is that they both seek to make the higher education curriculum more flexible, provide students with more choice, and offer alternative approaches to resource management. The use of either or both of them reflects institutional concerns about the marketability of their curriculum, as well as the efficient and effective organization of their resources. In the period of growth in student numbers in the late 1980s and early 1990s, promoted by a competitive funding regime (both internal and external to individual institutions), they both became crucial in the short to medium term. While some institutions may well have introduced them simply as insurance against the longer-term trends, others undoubtedly have developed them as possibly the only means to survival.

While higher education generally may have found itself with two potentially powerful tools with which to manage elements of the changes required to deliver a mass higher education system, institutions may use them in diverse ways dependent upon history, goals, personalities and pragmatism. In the change management process, this has often been far from clear to those who have experienced their introduction. This may not come as a surprise to observers of change in organizations generally. It is more surprising, and more disappointing, to realize that the implementers themselves have often fallen foul of the confusions. Too often the purpose of the exercise, the utility of the tools, has been initially unclear. This has been exacerbated by an increasingly hasty approach by which institutions have sought to change whole institutions very quickly. This book therefore seeks not only to look at how credit can change institutions, but also the models of change employed when they are introduced.

THE HISTORICAL DEVELOPMENT OF CREDIT-BASED SYSTEMS

The origins

The history of credit goes further back than is often assumed. While its emergence in the mid to late 1980s was a speedy process, the previous 20 years had seen a number of initiatives and an ongoing debate that provided the backcloth for subsequent activity. As far back as 1963 the Robbins Report itself pointed gently to the advantages of credit transfer. For those involved in the development of credit, there is a landscape of events, documents, people and activities over the last 25 years that have provided the platform for the current situation. These tend not to reflect a necessarily accurate history, but those features that have had the most impact, real or imagined, on the emergent system. Over the horizon of this landscape, there is the obvious exemplar of the US with its century-long history: a regular place of pilgrimage to those working with a new technology for which there was, for a long time, rarely any indigenous precedent.

Pioneers

The landmarks that are normally identified usually start with the Open University, though as often happens with the OU, its significant role in transforming higher education in the UK is often underestimated. This is partly because the later credit-based developments of the 1980s were founded on a very different credit tariff, and partly because, in terms of structures and markets, the OU and other universities were so radically different that there appeared, on the surface at least, little in common. But from its beginning in 1969, the principles of credit and modularity were built in and genuinely embedded into the student experience at the OU. In its attempts to open up access to adult students, and to concentrate on the needs of part-time students, it developed a model which many universities have begun to seriously imitate, at least in part, over the last decade. It is an irony that during the late 1980s the OU seemed in danger of losing its competitive advantage as it failed, like many innovators, to correctly judge the environment and the competition. The arrival of a new Vice-chancellor in the late 1980s has, however, led to the OU restoring its position, bringing itself into the mainstream of academic structures, and once again beginning to lead the way forward with, for example, its embracing of National Vocational Qualifications (NVQs). To many, however, the OU provides clues, in the way it uses its flexible academic structure, to the future shape of many higher education institutions. In this it has been exemplary in its use of credit as a means to an end – accessibility – rather than as an end in itself.

It is often conveniently forgotten that many of the old universities have, in one way or another, espoused some of the principles of modularity for a long time. Indeed, the Scottish higher education model is regarded as having informed the development of the US system. It has also been argued, for example, that Oxford itself was set up on the assumption of a unitized curriculum with students having to choose from across the institution. I myself studied on a faculty-based modular programme at one of the redbrick universities in the 1960s, starting out to study accountancy and ending up as an Africanist. While such a scheme may not have been institution-wide, it embraced, like many others, the notions of choice and flexibility.

Ernest Theodossin, in his excellent book *The Modular Market* (1986) gives some very good insights into how some of the modular schemes of the last 20 years were introduced. In particular, it shows how specific individuals and groups within institutions were crucial in instigating change. It is equally good at showing how often schemes like these failed to deliver what was intended because the right balance of needs between management, staff and students were not achieved. Some of this is dealt with in more detail in subsequent chapters, and the small outbreak of modularity in the 1970s and 1980s, involving polytechnics, now provides us with good case study material on the management of change. These initiatives provided a base line of practice for subsequent developments but ironically also provided a barrier to change. There are few people involved in the current development of either credit or modularity who have not regularly faced a barrage of criticism based on the real or perceived inadequacies of the 'Oxford Poly scheme' or the 'City of London scheme'. Indeed, a number of institutions have used the term 'unitization' deliberately to avoid any accusations that what was being introduced bore any relation to either of these schemes.

The CNAA

There was a great deal of talk in the late 1970s and early 1980s, but the next great surge in institutional activity did not occur until the mid-1980s. Here much of the talk came to fruition in a number of individual institutional initiatives, but in particular in the development of the CNAA CAT scheme. While this sought to provide a brokerage service for students and employers, its main significance lay in providing a national focus for development; a credit tariff that could be acceptable to most institutions; some early regulatory framework; development monies; and political clout. It gave many institutions, as well as people like me, both the tools and confidence to develop in ways that might not have happened, in the knowledge that the quality assurance structures of the CNAA would now support and encourage it. Robertson's criticisms of the CNAA, principally that it did not aid the development of a national and comprehensive credit framework, while technically correct, underestimate the way in which the pragmatism of the CNAA's approach very quickly provided a commonality of language and arithmetic that allowed individual institutions to pursue their own interests in the knowledge that there was a built-in flexibility and compatibility that would allow subsequent shifts in direction. As a result, while there was much that, retrospectively, the CNAA might have done differently, it remains the fact that without it the notion of a UK credit system would probably still remain a forlorn hope. The ultimate test of this has been the way in which the traditional universities have, however reluctantly, been willing to take on the CNAA's tariff.

Backed by the CNAA and other government agencies, the last half of the decade saw a range of credit-based initiatives in the then polytechnics. What is perhaps most significant, as will be explored later, is that while all were carried out under the same banner – normally CAT – they differed significantly in terms of structures, purpose and markets. Their particular significance was that they became a new baseline for further action, serving almost as an experimental laboratory developing good, and frequently bad, practice, but exploring some of the approaches as well as the limitations of credit-based systems. What was perhaps most different from the earlier initiatives, aside from the very different political and economic environment, was that credit, rather than modularity was the focus. Once again, the two were clearly interrelated but it was the idea of credit, and its inherent flexibilities for students, that captured the imagination of this particular group of practitioners.

The activities of this five-year period have subsequently set an agenda which is being worked through in the 1990s. Robertson, looking forward quizzically in his report to see whether there is the emergence of a 'culture of credit', notes that there is now a commitment on the part of most older universities towards extensive modularization; a continuing momentum among new universities towards the use of credits and/or modularity as organizing concepts of institutional life; and an active interest on the part of funding councils and others in using credit as a basis for rational resource management formulae, responsive to student choice.

While many, including Robertson himself, believe that the jury remains out on whether credit and modularity will, in the end, substantively change the nature of UK higher education, it is now the case that a significant majority of the expanded higher education sector has, in one way or another, taken on board their principles.

The international dimension

This experience of the UK over the last two decades in developing credit-based systems as it moves quickly to a mass higher education system is replicated to some extent on an international scale. As Robertson comments:

> *As nations come to expect more from the educational capacity of their citizens, an expansion of participation in higher education appears to be the global response. In most cases this has taken the form of increased diversity and flexibility, mediated by the introduction of credit-based and modular systems.* (p.286)

In a comprehensive survey of the international experience, he identified considerable development and some interesting patterns. Vigorous developments are occurring particularly in areas where either the culture of higher education has not yet been well developed, or where the changes to the education system also reflect an attempt to move away from the country's earlier history and associations. Notable among these are New Zealand and Australia, Thailand and the Philippines, India and Senegal. In continental Europe, two-thirds of European Union (EU) and European Free Trade Association (EFTA) countries have either a developing or a working credit system, and Eastern Europe in particular is showing considerable interest in using credit to transform its higher education institutions. However, within the European context, with the possible exception of Sweden, no country has developed so far as the UK in terms of modularity and credit. It is interesting to note, however, that some countries, unlike the UK, have used legal instruments to develop credit systems. This has happened, for example, in Spain, the Netherlands and Italy.

Other countries which are becoming involved are Vietnam, Singapore, South Korea, Japan and Malaysia. While much of the work in these countries is in an early stage of development, there is sufficient activity to strengthen the view that, whatever the individual circumstances of academic delivery, the tool of credit can have utility.

Robertson also notes, however, patterns of non-involvement in credit. In particular, countries where the higher education tradition is based on the German or French models do not seem to be developing along these lines. Nor, on the whole, are countries in Latin America, Africa and the Middle East. Robertson finds no one explanation for these patterns, though he is inclined in particular to view the possibility that 'new developments of credit systems throughout the world appear to be in countries which are seeking to escape from *élite formation* models, or do not wish to develop such models in the first place, or which are otherwise influenced by American practice'.

It remains the case, however, that at the international, as at the national, level there is no one model of credit, no dominant definition of credit, and no common system of levels. The US model remains the most powerful and emulated, and it remains the country of pilgrimage for those wishing to introduce credit-based systems, though it made a refreshing change when in 1995 I was visited by the Vice-chancellor of a Lithuanian University who was on a UK study tour seeking advice on the development of credits and semesters. However, while the principles may be copied the practice is almost always customized rather than replicated.

For the UK practitioner, it is interesting to note some recent interest in the model being developed in New Zealand. The specific interest here is in the attempts of the New Zealand Qualifications Authority (NZQA) to develop a comprehensive national credit framework unifying further and higher, vocational and non-vocational education. For many UK practitioners the scale and scope of the exercise (which includes plans for a national database and a student record system) provides the sort of framework that could resolve many of the institutional issues they face. Somewhat depressingly, however, Robertson concludes that its does not appear that 'the Universities in New Zealand are prepared to embrace the credit framework as readily as its proposals suggest'.

More optimistically, it may well be the UK system, whatever its inadequacies, which may become the focus for international interest. The last few years have seen a number of visitors from continental Europe and further beyond seeking to determine whether the UK model held anything out for them. In the end, despite the substantial variations in the nature of the credit systems across the world, there appear to be two things that are shared. First, the underpinning principle of increasing flexibility for both student and University. Secondly, the sheer difficulty of introducing credit-based systems at institutional and national levels. The latter is best expressed by a quote based on experience in Lesotho, but which would be universally recognizable to the international network of credit practitioners. In his report for the World Bank on academic credit systems Omporn Regel, warning about the long period of change required and the dangers of hybrid models, commented:

> *At the National University of Lesotho... initial efforts to combine academic aspects of British academic requirements with a modified American academic credit system have created a complex and hybrid programme.... Excessive faculty time has also been absorbed in administration and paperwork at the expense of teaching and research. It is important to realise that the development of the credit system in America took place over a long period of time, and the system continuously responded to other factors which helped form contemporary American Universities.*
>
> (Regel, 1992)

Models of modularity

As has been shown, the distinction between modularity and credit as tools rather than specific products, and as means rather than ends, is not always clearly understood within higher education. For many people, initial perceptions, reactions and resistances are centred on the actual products of these tools, for example a CAT scheme or a modular scheme. These are perceived as coming ready-built; are seemingly delivered from on high; and may appear to be imposed from outside the institution. It is therefore important that those involved in both introducing and delivering the new systems should understand the variety of models and the purpose underlying the introduction of one or other of them. The following framework is not intended to be definitive but allows current and future practice to be analysed and evaluated.

The simplest level at which modularity can work is one at which a single course or academic award is broken down into self-contained components (not necessarily equal in size) which are separately assessed. Such a course may be described as *module-based.* It is much more common throughout the sector than is normally acknowledged. The next, and quite common, level is where students on a module-based course or degree, can take options (similarly self-contained) from other courses/awards. In the sense that this enables students to move beyond the boundaries of a specific course, this may be said to be a *modular course*. It might be that, building on the development of modular courses, a Department or Faculty – a group of cognate subjects – then chooses to coordinate its activities and allow students to move more easily within this group, and to design more complex programmes of study, including major/minor combinations. This could be, though usually isn't, called a *departmental* or *faculty modular scheme.*

These first three levels are fairly common within all higher education institutions, and are not even regarded as 'modular' by many of their practitioners. They are often seen as a healthy extension of the disciplinary base, and frequently emerge from the interests and inclinations of staff themselves. In general these three uses of *modules* and *modularity* need not be particularly problematic to academic practitioners either in academic, management, or administrative terms because they do not threaten the autonomy of subject or disciplinary groups.

The major break for institutions, however, is in allowing students to move across departmental or faculty boundaries. It appears to be a logical, evolutionary stage for departments or faculties which are close relations to start interacting. However, while it does occur, the managerial and administrative requirements of such a move often limit it. The achievement of an *institutionally based modular scheme* that genuinely breaks down faculty and departmental boundaries usually requires central action.

The institutionally based modular scheme can take various forms. For example, an institution can break down all (or a large proportion) of its existing provision into self-contained blocks. Such blocks may, but do not necessarily have to be, of a standard size. How these blocks are utilized, regulated, and managed might then be left to the discretion of institutional sub-units such as faculties or departments. At its most minimal level, this can be described as a *modularized* or *unitized institution* where the tool has been delivered, but no specific institution-wide outcomes identified. An extension of that model is where substantial devolution is retained, but is managed within an agreed set of institution-wide regulations that ensures consistency in terms of assessment, progression and other matters. This is sometimes described as an *academic framework*. However, because students are still admitted to faculties or departments, and principally managed by them, it can be called a *devolved institutional modular scheme*.

The final level is where most of the management and administrative functions are highly centralized and where, in effect, the student enters the institution and the scheme, rather than a department/faculty. This *institutional modular scheme* is the purest model, though rather rarer than is assumed. To many people, unfortunately, this is the model that they understand when the term *modularity* is used. It is also the model that is managerially closest to the archetypal US university where, while credit is important, the central organizing principle (though not the term) is modularity.

The list is imperfect and the categories overdrawn. But it represents the broad options available within the modular model. While theoretically an institution could move from module-based courses to an institutional modular scheme, the practice is more complex, with some institutions starting at different points; and with separate parts of an institution moving in different ways, and at a different pace. In the current climate, in particular, some institutions will miss out most levels, or at least move more quickly through them. Additionally each level may be an end-point for an institution or one of its sub-units.

The history of the development of flexible structures has generally been centred around the principle of, if not the term, modularity. However, built into many such developments has been the concept of credit. Indeed, virtually by definition, modularity cannot work without some notion of credit. However, the tariffs that were used to support early institutional modular schemes were usually internal to a particular institution and crudely based around single/double/treble combinations, given that complete standardization across an institution has been very rare. Credit in this sense, then, has been mostly about the internal accumulation of modules.

Models of credit

The last decade, however, has seen the emergence of a more complex and sophisticated view of credit. At a broad level, the rising significance of credit was initially based on issues relating to transfer, principally the transfer of credits between institutions and, subsequently, between a variety of learning situations which did not necessarily involve either educational institutions or formal education. As such the important issue was the development of a credit tariff that would provide an inter-institutional currency.

Given the existence of such a tariff, now virtually universal within higher education, a number of institutional models have emerged. They are neither tidy nor exclusive, but represent ways in which the tool of credit is used. At the most basic level, existing modularized provision within an institution might be measured in terms of the credit tariff. More importantly, an institution going through the process of modularizing from scratch might evade the issue of standardization (often a major barrier to gaining staff support) by utilizing the tariff and therefore bringing together a wide range of differentially sized units.

More significantly, an institution can set up a separate CAT unit and CAT scheme. Here a centrally organized unit accepts students as CAT students, who are assisted in devising a programme of study, having had their prior learning (formal or experiential) assessed, and having gained appropriate exemptions. The programme devised for students might be based on existing units within the mainstream full-time provision of the university; or might incorporate specifically offered/designed modules.

Even more radically, the institution can devise a set of progression and award regulations based upon credit, along the lines of the CNAA CAT regulations. This becomes the framework for all provision within the institution. As with modularity this can still leave many decisions and mechanisms in the hands of institutional sub-units, and offers a range of options. For example, mechanisms for the assessment of prior learning (APL) can be used to provide credit rating for off-campus learning (employer/work-based); for experience; and for certificated learning. This maximizes opportunities for advanced standing against awards offered by the institutional sub-units. Similarly, sub-units within an institution may work with partner organizations such as employers to provide in-house programmes; other educational or training bodies to provide regionally or nationally based programmes; or colleges to enable cross-sector mobility. More radically, the institution's regulations can allow staff to reorganize their curriculum offer so that more flexible opportunities are offered, including customized and combined routes. Here it is likely that the principles of credit and modularity will become integrated, and possibly indistinguishable.

The most radical option is found where an institution deliberately integrates its credit and modular principles at an institutional level to maximize student opportunities to bring credit with them (and take it away), and maximize the student's ability to negotiate their own programme of study within the institution. In this sort of situation, rarely if ever achieved, the two tools are brought together to enhance each other's advantages.

Credit can therefore be used separately, or in combination with modularity, to serve a number of objectives that an institution may wish to achieve. It remains the case, however, that the great power of credit, and its undoubted advantage over modularity, is that it can more easily work across institutions; between different sites of learning; and between different types and size of learning experience. It can have a international, national and regional function, as well as enhancing internal institutional flexibility.

However, the debate that sometimes occurs about modularity *versus* credit is in essence a red herring. For certain strategic purposes within institutions, they are separate issues; for others they are helpful and complementary tools.

Change in the further education sector

A principal (and hardly surprising) conclusion of the Robertson Report was that one of the most critical requirements is a national credit framework that would embrace all post-16 (and possibly post-14) education. Robertson's view is that the means to achieve this would be the use of a definition of credit that attributed one credit to every 30 hours of learning, for a long time the principal building block of the Open College Networks (OCNs), and more recently for the Further Education Unit's (FEU) model of credit. This has been the focus for one of the more hard-fought theological-style disputes within higher education credit practitioners, many of whom would be reluctant to lose the advantages gained by the establishment of the CNAA's 120 credits/year tariff.

Most, however, would welcome the clear signs that many further education colleges look set to establish the principles of credit and modularity at the heart of institutional life. The strong links formed between further and higher education over the past few years, with students able to study for university awards in their local college, or transfer credits into a higher education institution, make some of this an obvious next step. However, as with higher education, rapid growth, incorporation, and a particular funding council methodology, have been an even stronger influence. 1994, in particular, saw major strides in certain areas with the development of a unitized Wales; the establishment, with the support of £250,000 from the Single Regeneration Budget, of a London CAT Consortium; and a proliferation of unitization projects throughout the UK. What may be of more significance is to see that what appears to be part of Robertson's view of ultimate convergence of the different credit frameworks now being used in the UK, may be the first seeds of divergence. The articulation that further education appears to be seeking, initially at least, is not so much with higher education, but with NCVQ.

Unitization in further education

Thus the concept of unitization has a very different meaning within further education and is neither a euphemism for, or an alternative to, modularization. It is, in crude terms, the identification in the abstract of a set of learning outcomes, to which can be given an arithmetic value and a level derived from the Further Education Unit's credit model. Once units have been approved, for example by an Open College Network, institutions are then free to incorporate them into their curriculum in whatever way they feel is most appropriate. Units, or groups of units, might then be turned into modules as the means of delivering and managing the curriculum. The distinction between the unit as the definer of the curriculum, and the module as the means of its delivery is therefore quite clear. This model bears some resemblance to the NCVQ framework, with which it shares some compatible assumptions. It is in one sense a purer and less pragmatic model of credit than exists in higher education.

It is still far too early to identify what will be the advantages and disadvantages of such a purist stance. The national management of this unitized curriculum will undoubtedly present some interesting challenges. But in the short to medium term it does seem to make more problematic the convergence, and even the articulation, of the further and higher education credit systems. It is no longer a question of common or compatible tariffs, but of a different underpinning philosophy.

However, in general terms, the further education sector faces many of the same debates, issues, struggles and battles that have been taxing higher education over the last decade. As such, much of what will be said, might well apply to further education colleges. The managerial skills required to deliver such a complex agenda, both nationally and locally, will be the same.

A revolution or a passing fad?

In his report Robertson claims that:

> *progress in higher and further education demonstrates unambiguous continuity of purpose in the pursuit of credit systems and a national credit framework. This is evident from policy-makers, senior institutional administrators and, where given the opportunity, from academic colleagues themselves.*

While acknowledging that many still see credit as a passing phase, an ideological conspiracy, or an administrative irrelevance, he noted both the existence of substantial change, and the need for further significant developments.

Robertson himself, despite being in recent years a dominant public figure in this field, is sceptical of too many claims about the current centrality and universality of credit or modularity. He believes, reluctantly, that much of the apparent change might well be superficial, and inadequately embedded in genuinely changed institutional practice. He is very aware that the strong external policy environment is rarely supported by equally strong support from the academic staff within institutions, and warns about underestimating the power of academics to resist change. He is concerned that the student experience, and particularly the element of choice within that, is being tinkered with rather than transformed. But, despite this he recognizes substantial momentum for change.

The increasing significance of credit is reflected in a number of ways. Funding agencies are now taking a strong interest in how credit might facilitate a more sensitive funding methodology. Similarly, while the existence of three apparently competing credit structures (CNAA, FEU and NCVQ), is a matter of concern to Robertson, the very existence of such competition is suggestive of considerable change. And, while they may have different motives, a majority of institutions throughout the higher education sector now appear to have committed themselves to a variety of change packages which include variations on the themes of modularization (and semesterization) and the acceptance of the CNAA credit tariff.

All this suggests an overall momentum that will increasingly provide a credit-based national framework within which institutions might adhere to the general principles and structures of a credit-based system, while pursuing radically different paths through this framework. In this, of course, the UK would be no different from the US where a national credit model can cope with, and indeed encourages and allows, differences between, say, Princeton and the local community college. The general realization and acceptance that a credit framework does not imply or demand uniformity and standardization except at a limited threshold level, would constitute a major breakthrough for credit-based systems.

Chapter 3

Managing the Flexible Institution

Robert Allen

PIONEERING DEVELOPMENTS

Introduction

In 1988, I wrote that if credit is 'merely a totem for change, it will undoubtedly do more harm than good' (Allen, 1988). At that time, CAT was one of several terms coming into fashion – 'enterprise', for example, was another buzz-word just beginning to attract controversy – and it seemed perfectly possible that credit could be just another 'here today, gone tomorrow' idea. At the time, however, it was attracting some rather cultish attention and the previous five years had seen several institutional, regional and national initiatives, particularly within the polytechnic sector. The CNAA CAT unit had been set up; a small number of institutions had introduced limited schemes; and there had emerged various consortia. Predictably, an attendant conference/workshop circuit had been opened up. The cult members were usually polytechnic academics, maybe with some middle-level institutional role: the now ubiquitous CAT coordinator was already beginning to appear. As we have seen, the 'movement' had some eminent gurus. With the arrival of the CNAA CAT regulations in 1986, there was also a biblical text.

What schemes there were tended to be marginal to institutions, in terms of both impact and funding. They were often pilot projects, supported by external funding from government agencies such as the Manpower Services Commission (MSC). They also tended to be directed at marginal groups of students as with, for example, the Associate Student Schemes at the University of Central Lancashire and the University of Northumbria at Newcastle, or the company-based schemes at Greenwich and Portsmouth Universities. They were, however, crucial in allowing institutions and individuals within them to begin to introduce both the concepts and practices of credit. They provided limited experimental situations, which allowed experience and expertise to be developed without causing too much damage. More importantly, such limited schemes, when they worked, provided role models for the ideas to be spread throughout the institution. Additionally, these early schemes became the basis for the development of nationwide practice.

But it was still the case that, outside of a very small group of proponents, there remained within the academic community at worst ignorance and at best a considerable level of suspicion and scepticism. Less than a decade later, while much scepticism remains, there are many more institutions and individuals designing and delivering credit-based schemes. In this chapter I will look at the way in which institutions have attempted during this period to take on and incorporate credit-based schemes despite the resistances, and the structures and the mechanisms they have introduced to utilize their potential.

Early initiatives

Without romanticizing them, the early practitioners were put in the position of being pioneers and evangelists. In their own institutions they were likely, if known at all, to be seen as cranky or irrelevant, and often both. Picked for their enthusiasm and assumed thick skins, the members of this group were effectively faced with the task – not always clear even to them – of changing the culture of an institution. For this role – the archetypal 'change agent' of 1980s management literature – they were often formally, and sometimes blissfully, unprepared. Nor did they have many opportunities to learn from the experience of others because there were very few established or successful precedents. Visits to the few institutions with emerging credit schemes was one option open to us, and the Sheffields, Lancashires and Newcastles of the CAT world received constant pilgrimages. What was notable was the level of openness and cooperation and the willingness to give advice and support. Possibly because they were institutionally marginal, the credit practitioners sought to strengthen their external links. As a result, consistency and good practice, the essence of a national credit system, was disseminated more quickly than might have been anticipated.

The CNAA, similarly, was always available as a source of information and advice and the CAT unit saw itself as having a staff development role. Its officers moved around on a roadshow basis, developing the national network and establishing consistency across institutions. The consortia, in particular, acted as practitioner networks, sometimes offering staff development, but serving a subsidiary role as a combination of club and self-help therapy group. A number of individuals naturally turned to the US for role models: a procession of such people followed (literally!) Norman Evans of the Learning from Experience Trust on his voyages through US east coast community colleges and universities attempting to establish as quickly as possible the basic parameters and practices for credit-based systems. The institutional developments of the following years did not therefore take place in a vacuum. Internal change was often predicated on an emerging national context and consensus, often invisible to individuals working within institutions, but managed and mediated by a strong practitioner network.

Despite some emergent commonality across institutions, however, there was frequently a strong sense of the blind leading the blind. There was plenty of rhetoric, and an abundance of sophisticated theory, but in reality institutional practice was limited to the experience of the Open University and the few modular structures around the country that had emerged in the 1970s. Even in the late 1980s the examples of substantial and successful activity were limited to a small number of institutions.

CAT and modularity

There are of course strong links between modularity and credit, as has been shown in Chapter 2. But initially CAT, as it quickly had become known, was something very different to modularity. In the eyes of its proponents, it was designed to do things that modularity couldn't. Some CAT practitioners were, indeed, individuals who had become disillusioned by the lack of flexibility that they perceived in supposedly flexible modular structures. Pioneer modular schemes such as the ones at the University of Hertfordshire and Oxford Brookes University were seen as not having broken the mould of what Norbert Singer, a noted proponent of credit, had called the 'tyranny of the three-year degree'. Indeed, Ernest Theodossin (1986) went as far as to suggest that Oxford Brookes University's modular scheme had, by the mid-1980s moved 'back towards the condition from which it was intended to represent a departure' and had not delivered a genuinely student-centred model of the curriculum. Many believed that the modular schemes were still essentially managerial structures which, while allowing students some more choice, were specifically designed to enable the institutions to be managed differently.

For many of the early CAT practitioners, the agenda was to put the student genuinely at the centre of the institutional universe, and introduce 'consumer choice' as the most significant feature of academic programmes. Their views were summed up in a speech made by Roger Waterhouse, then of Wolverhampton University, and later to become the Vice-chancellor of the University of Derby, when he said:

> *The discourse of the 'course' reinforces its tyranny with the rhetoric of integration, coherence and progression. Within the confines of that discourse, to say that the course must go is to advocate disintegration, incoherence and lack of progression. But it is never the course which is integrated, coherent and progressive – if anything it is the student's learning experience.*

Preaching and practice

As such, CAT was seen as genuinely putting the student at the forefront to the extent that it was possible to give them credit even if they did not physically attend the institution granting the credit. The early proponents were very much concerned with student empowerment: with what students had done and wanted to do. Ultimately, it was argued, only students could define what was 'coherent and progressive' for them.

This clarity of purpose was the strength of this group of practitioners. It would also be a weakness because, sometimes by default and sometimes deliberately, this view placed the staff of their institution, and particularly the academic staff, in what could be perceived (with some legitimacy) as a secondary, service role. Somebody's so-called 'empowerment' usually means that someone else loses power. Stressing the primacy of the students is a view that can go down a storm at a conference of CAT practitioners, but merely create one when the participant returns home, threatening as it does the power and control of academic staff.

It was also the case that the views held by these practitioners were sometimes underpinned by quite different motives from the ones held by their institutional sponsors, to whom wider political and resource agendas were behind the sudden enthusiasm for CAT. This was of course the period of the (retrospectively) bemusing panic over demographic downturn, when it was thought that the number of 18-year old applicants would decrease dramatically, and that the key to recruitment and therefore survival would have to be new, adult-based, markets. Most CAT practitioners understood that, though the means were the same for both themselves and their superiors, the ends might be entirely different. But equally, they were happy to accept and take advantage of the fact that CAT might be one of the few educational concepts which could prove attractive to both educational philosophers and resource managers.

Managing upwards

The nature and position of this early group of middle-level practitioners within the polytechnics is important in understanding subsequent developments. It has become fashionable within management theory to identify certain 'change agents' who have the ability to 'manage up' the system, creating the conditions and mechanisms for change. Such a model is seen as a desirable way of ensuring that change in organizations is maximized because those at the lower levels of the hierarchy can see themselves as owning, and even initiating, change. Genuine change, the argument goes, cannot be imposed from above.

While there is some attraction in such a view and it is undoubtedly the case that some of the early CAT practitioners had the required qualities and skills to introduce change, many of those same practitioners would not recognize in themselves the exciting and liberating world of the management guru's change agent. Instead they were more likely to feel trapped between the indifference and insensitivity of the senior manager, and the hostility of academic, and often administrative, staff. It is clear that if they were to be successful, much depended on the way in which they were managed 'down'. The nature of such downward management is an issue we will return to later in this chapter.

It is important to remember that the response of individuals within institutions can be highly variable, and managers must beware of homogenizing either academic or administrative staff. Robertson handily categorizes academic staff in terms of their approach to the introduction of credit-based systems. He identifies four groups: the enthusiasts, whose commitment is based on a 'crusade' for access, democratic participation and institutional reform; the pragmatists, who look at and sometimes find in credit answers to the practical problems they face; the sceptics who, while questioning the purposes and processes, seek to balance educational change with familiar academic practice; and the antagonists who, in general, reject the whole enterprise (1994, p.314). It tends, of course to be the latter group on which change managers usually focus. The reality is that it is the expansion and development of the first three groups that is crucial to change.

Despite the problems, by 1993 the marginal cult had become competitive with the mainstream. According to various sources, 80 per cent of *all* universities (not just the old polytechnics) were moving into credit-based structures and the vast majority had formally attached themselves to the CNAA credit tariff. A model of a credit-based higher education system had apparently begun to emerge within the UK. Such a rapid movement puts the individuals we have been talking about into perspective. Instead of seeing them as a cult who forced change on to the system, it could be argued that, all along, the UK higher education system was a credit system in waiting. One way or another, institutions would have had to change dramatically to cope with the rapid move from an élite to a mass system. CAT, along with modularity, were simply convenient and possibly predictable tools. The CAT practitioners were merely the front-line troops. As such, they were important in introducing change but the real force lay in the way those who managed the system, internal and external to institutions, saw the resolution of the essential dilemma: how to fund and organize a mass higher education system on continuously reducing resources.

STRATEGIC CONSIDERATIONS

Why and how?

Given the range of models available, the major issue facing higher education institutions wishing to introduce credit-based schemes, is *why* and *how* one or more of the available models might be introduced. Unfortunately, but perhaps predictably, these questions are not always asked at the beginning of the process or, if they are, the answers are rarely handed on explicitly to those who must deliver the changed structures.

Two sets of reasons are usually identified as underlying the introduction of credit and/or modularity. Perhaps inevitably, though certainly not helpfully, they are normally grouped under the banners of 'educational' and 'managerial'. The educational reasons proposed include: increased flexibility for students; interdisciplinary opportunities for both staff and students; educational breadth as well as depth; empowerment of students; curriculum development; introduction of skills components to academic courses; enhancing vocational relevance through introduction of secondary subjects; student-centred learning; and attractiveness to mature students, particularly through the development of part-time courses.

The managerial reasons, at least as perceived by many academics, include: larger classes; higher student–staff ratios; staff rationalization; the breaking down of disciplinary closed shops; disempowerment of academic staff; increased centralized managerial control; curriculum control.

It would of course be foolish, given the resource climate of the last few years, to suggest that the recent surge towards modularity and credit is not directly connected to the need of higher education institutional managers to find more cost-effective forms of delivery. Secondly, all of the above explanations (some of which overlap) could well feature even within one institution. As such the educational and managerial reasons are not necessarily mutually exclusive. Indeed, as has already been stressed, it may be the strength of modularity and credit that they can meet the needs of those who would promote educational change as well as those seeking managerial efficiency and effectiveness.

The early examples of the introduction of CAT might better help us understand the options and dilemmas than current developments can. More recently, the rapid move of institutions into the credit/modular/semester model involves a less prolonged, more directed, and frequently less reflective process. It is more clearly centrally determined, and the internal debates and battles, while remaining, take place within a situation that results from the clear, and often hasty, imposition of change from above. This is not, however it appears, inevitable, and the consequences may be the subject of considerable regret in the future. Yet it would be fair to say that, in the current climate, managers may understandably feel that they have no choice and no time, and that their only option is speedy, top-down imposition of new structures.

The earlier developments varied more in style and content, and threw up more complex managerial issues and processes, simply because there was not necessarily any sense of inevitability about them, and, as long as most institutions remained outside of the system, there still remained an apparent element of choice.

It is important to acknowledge that the methods of introducing credit schemes have varied considerably. What is not always understood, and this is frequently a barrier to change, is that diversity is a strong feature of credit-based systems. The tenaciously held view that credit and modularity come in standard forms is simply not supported by the evidence. From the mid-1980s onwards, a number of institutions developed credit-based arrangements for at least some of their students. But what was done, and the way it was done, depended on a range of factors specific to the institutions and individuals involved. Resources, geography, history, personalities and other institutional circumstances all had their effect on the nature of specific developments. It is interesting that many of the early practitioners had Continuing Education or Access backgrounds, and their underlying motives for developing schemes usually related to the widening of access to socially, economically and educationally underprivileged groups rather than simply a response to the need to grow. The emphasis that was often put on the *transfer* element of CAT was linked to views that it was the adult, and educationally underprivileged, would-be student that had most to gain from CAT. The pioneering Associate Student Scheme at the University of Northumbria at Newcastle, probably the first major credit scheme in the UK outside of the OU and funded by over £150,000 from the Manpower Services Commission, was just such a development. Similarly, the LINCS scheme at the University of Central Lancashire, set up about the same time, aimed at attracting people into local colleges with the possibility of subsequently transferring their credits into the University. These two schemes, which provided my own first experience of credit, had a genuine sense of not only being a new tool, but of actually opening up higher education in a radical way. For me, and many of my peers, they were not only to prove the utility of credit in making institutions more flexible, but also to provide a sense of vision and purpose to the exercise.

Credit in practice: case studies

One of the origins of this book was a debate among practitioners as to what was the 'best' model for developing credit-based institutions. At that time in the early 1990s, Liverpool John Moores University had achieved some prominence as being at the leading edge in credit-based developments, and had become the favoured spot for pilgrims. Its attraction lay in the very radical stance it had taken with the introduction of its Integrated Credit Scheme (ICS). While its prominence was partly tied into the national profile of the scheme's inventor and Director, David Robertson, it was clearly at that time the best example of what had come to be known as the 'big-bang' approach, though Wolverhampton University had begun to come close to developing both credit and modularity comprehensively at an institutional level. At Liverpool, however, there was an attempt from the very beginning to provide a major synthesis, fusing credit, modularity and an outcomes-led curriculum. Directed and managed strongly from the centre of the institution, it sought to move at a rapid pace to incorporate the whole of the academic programme of the university into a credit-based modular framework. Highly centralized and sophisticated management and administrative functions, well supported through mainstream funding, were set up bringing together registry, management information, and guidance functions. Schools within the university 'contracted' with the scheme to provide modules, fields and routes, with the central managers of the scheme coordinating and managing the provision according to student demand. It was, in the words of its Director, an attempt 'to embark upon a sustained and radical programme of institutional transformation which would bring the institution quickly forward on a broad front of sector innovations' (Robertson, 1994, p.66).

Introduced in 1989, the scheme was frequently contrasted with earlier, more partial and less ambitious, schemes. Two of these were themselves very contrasting approaches developed by two other well-known pioneers of credit, Sheffield Hallam University and the University of Greenwich. Indeed, it was these contrasts and debates and our personal experiences that first stimulated this book. I, in particular, despite an intellectual proclivity to assume that there was never a 'right' way, had become firmly attached to the view that 'big-bang'models, which appeared to be increasingly the vogue, could never work.

Greenwich and Liverpool appeared in fact to be at opposite ends of the spectrum with the former, as we shall later see, taking an extremely prolonged approach. On the surface, Sheffield Hallam University looked to be somewhere in the middle of this spectrum. It had moved into the CAT arena in 1988 in a way that was probably seen by many practitioners at that earlier time as the most desirable route. A separate CAT unit was set up with its own scheme and staff. It facilitated the delivery of individualized programmes of study for students wishing to pursue their own unique interests. In this way the University admitted and administered a cohort of CAT students whose home was within the CAT unit, even though their studies took place within 'modules' derived from the university's mainstream courses. The university's ability to do this, and its leadership as a CAT institution, was based on a major coup in attracting funding for 150 students from the funding body. This was to be unique and created an extremely strong base for pursuing a fairly pure model of CAT, which genuinely put power into the hands of incoming students. In this way the University was able to develop a strong Combined Studies programme, and develop strong links with employers and professional bodies through the accreditation of work-based learning. Thus this was a highly centralized model, but it served as an alternative to, and was marginal to, mainstream delivery. It contrasted with both the devolution of Greenwich and the mainstream centralization of Liverpool.

My own institution, the University of Greenwich, on the other hand, had moved in a very different way. Although having one of the first validated institutional CAT schemes in the UK, it initially focused its energies on Continuing Professional Development. Indeed, a central CAT unit was never set up, and less than a dozen students ever passed through the central CAT Scheme. Instead, the University concerned itself with the way in which credit could be attached to professionally oriented training and experience in order to maximize accessibility to higher education awards. Though this partly reflected preferences on the part of a number of people within the university, there was a very strong pragmatic element relating to available funding opportunities. The university had been involved in a project, funded by the CNAA and MSC, which looked in some detail at the mechanisms for the accreditation of in-company training. At that time there was a major debate about how universities could get closer to the workplace, and provide more opportunities for professional development and updating. We were able to sell the idea that credit would produce the flexibility to make this happen, and we were therefore able to utilize government-sponsored funding from the PICKUP initiative to develop and mainstream the credit model. As a result, the emphasis in the early days was on the development of a more flexible postgraduate/post-experience structure which could grant credit for a range of activities, including various forms of formal and informal continuing professional development. Though a parallel process of unitization was introduced, this was seen as a separate and longer-term exercise. In both cases, while managed from the centre, this was a model that stressed facilitation, development and devolution.

The developments at Sheffield Hallam and Greenwich, while substantial, and ultimately highly significant, were therefore initially marginal and required specialized, non-mainstream funding. The debate that emerged nationally, which came to be focused around the experiment at Liverpool, was whether accretional developmental models, situated on the edge of institutions, and developed over relatively long periods of time, could ever successfully provide the base for transforming an institution. The answer from Liverpool at that stage was clearly no, and the ICS was an expression of a belief that transformation required a radical, centralized, root and branch approach. This was attractive to many, not simply because it looked very impressive, but also because increasingly individuals were being asked by senior managers to deliver mainstream credit-based systems more quickly. The luxury that, for example, Greenwich had, of having time to change, was fast disappearing.

Similar goals: alternative models

The differences between these three models reflect differences in institutional histories and missions; the management philosophies and styles of the senior institutional managers; and, to some extent, the backgrounds and personalities of the practitioners themselves. One thing that all had in common, however, was an institutional leader who was well known nationally for commitment to credit. In that sense, all three institutions were clearly and publicly committed to credit as a potential vehicle for considerable structural and cultural change.

The three institutions had very specific sets of circumstances that influenced both their reasons for developing credit and, to some extent, the way they did it. Sheffield Hallam had a highly structured, single honours programme, which was strongly vocationally oriented and centred on sandwich degrees. These had proved highly resistant to any introduction of flexibility and choice. At Greenwich, there was a Vice-chancellor with a history of introducing modularity in other institutions, and a sense of frustration at not being able to open up, except in patches, his current institution. Neither, however, seem to have felt the need, or been inclined, to take on their institution directly with root and branch change and sought instead to create conditions for change through a more indirect route. Liverpool, on the other hand, had come through a turbulent period when its very existence had been threatened. It was keen to re-establish its viability and credibility, and seems to have sought a new start.

At the time these three models and variations of them were reflected in other institutions developing credit-based systems, provided a focus for a general debate about change which tended to be based around the dichotomies of 'big-bang versus incrementalist' and 'top-down versus bottom-up' models of change. While analytically helpful, like all ideal types, they oversimplify. All three institutions relied heavily on strong leadership from the top, and were careful to ensure that individuals and resources were put in place to implement the goals that had been identified at the top. All three were quite clear in their view of the need in the medium to long term to radically alter the structures by which the academic programmes were delivered. Time scales and processes may have differed, but none stands up to any romanticized notions of grass-roots, bottom-up change. Where they did differ was in the model of how people could be made to change. Each model made different assumptions about what was needed to bring about changes in attitudes and working practices.

If one looks carefully, they all started with a similar assumption: that most people would resist change. Crudely put, the initial response to that assumption varied between a view that people should be made to change (Liverpool); that people who wanted change should, initially at least, have their own structures (Sheffield); and that people should be persuaded, for whatever reasons and by whatever means, to change (Greenwich). Once again, this overdraws the contrast, and also the clarity with which these views were held. But there is sufficient in it to see how common goals were thought to require very different approaches to achieving them.

It is tempting to make judgements about these three models. Before attributing virtue to any of them, however, it is worth remembering that management style, institutional circumstance, and pragmatism almost certainly played a stronger role than management theory in determining the tactics adopted within the different institutions.

The benefit of hindsight

It is also interesting to note that, while the contrast between the three institutions was a very useful device even as late as 1992, history has subsequently had its toll. All three institutions have shifted their tactics considerably, though it remains difficult without the benefit of sufficient information to calculate what led to these changes. The national circumstances, for example, have changed with consolidation of student numbers rather than dramatic growth, the keynote for all institutions. All three institutions seem to remain committed to their original strategy, but none could say that they have yet achieved it. At Liverpool, now five years on, there have been substantial changes in approach. David Robertson, who himself experienced the explosions that accompany 'big bangs', commented in his report that the Liverpool model was 'arguably in advance of institutional capacity to manage' and that 'institutional reorganisation complicated authority roles'. Hidden beneath this generous, and carefully coded, analysis lies a reality in which Liverpool's impressively centralized and sophisticated structures failed in their original intentions because they were not supported by key institutional players at senior and middle management levels. Such a model of change will always lead to such a battle, and while defeat is by no means inevitable, it requires considerable commitment, tenacity and skill to see through the inevitable disturbances. Despite this, Robertson is able to comment that the scheme 'remains institution-wide and developing, but with regressions, problems of scale and some unfilled potential' (1994, p.67).

Before those who oppose big bang models feel too smug, however, Robertson's last comment about the current state of play at Liverpool could equally apply to the current situation at both Sheffield Hallam and Greenwich or, indeed, any other institution that has introduced credit-based systems within the last decade. While both have seen considerable expansion of credit and modularity and could justifiably say that the principles would apply institution-wide, both have faced problems in exploiting the full potential of these tools. Indeed, both possibly remain better known for the way that they have used credit externally, than for the internal exploitation of the modular schemes they have introduced. While their phased approach has caused relatively less disturbance and ensured continuity of purpose, it also brings with it different problems requiring resolution.

Greenwich, in particular, has experienced a disjuncture between the academic development aspect of change, and the development of administrative systems to support it. While much has changed, and the tools of credit and modularity have undoubtedly extended choice on a number of fronts, the essentially devolved approach led to levels of patchiness and incompatibility that could have threatened the viability of the scheme, and certainly dismayed a new Vice-chancellor. Sheffield, on the other hand, which has strongly supported, in resource and systems terms the development and expansion of its combined studies programme, and is particularly strong on the guidance element, would probably still not claim that the mainstreaming of high levels of flexibility and choice has yet been achieved. Both would probably feel, on balance, that the approach they had adopted was the right approach, but would wish that there was an easier and shorter way.

Some of the elements of these case studies will be explored in more detail in Chapters 4 and 6. While circumstances may have changed, both nationally and within the three institutions themselves, in their initial form the case studies expose some of the range of techniques available for implementing change within higher education institutions. Other universities and colleges have gone along similar paths with differing degrees of success. Cheltenham and Gloucester College looks like an example of a big-bang model that has succeeded, whereas the shock waves continue to resound around the rapid changes at the University of Nottingham. Other institutions such as Middlesex University and the University of Central Lancashire, seemed to have arrived over a long period of time, and with relatively low levels of turbulence, at a position of high levels of flexibility. Ironically, some of the early pioneers such as the University of Northumbria at Newcastle and the University of Portsmouth have in recent times revisited the subject, having failed to establish significant change first time around.

History repeating itself: the case of continuing education?

The voluntary model of change, with institutions choosing to take the credit-based route, that was a feature of the mid to late 1980s seems to have been replaced, superficially at least, in the 1990s by an apparent belief that all but a few institutions have little choice but to go along the route of modularity and credit. Both the reports of Gaie Davidson (1992) and Robertson show public commitment to such change on the part of a large majority of traditional universities. While the suspicion remains that some of this might be cosmetic or preventive, preparing for the unanticipated, Davidson suggests that many of these institutions are now managed by a younger generation of Vice-chancellors who are committed to systematic change and will understand the utility of the tools of modularity and credit in delivering this.

This commitment may well have been enhanced by the changes imposed by the Higher Education Funding Council (HEFC) in 1994 on continuing education within the traditional universities. This shift, over a relatively limited time-scale, into a credit-based and credit-funded framework, raises many of the same issues relating to marginality and resistance as was experienced by early CAT practitioners. Indeed, in many senses the problems faced are more difficult, given that choice has not been an option and many of those required to implement the changes have strong philosophical aversions to them. This is 'big-bang' not only from the top, but from outside, with little consultation and extremely tight time-scales. Added to this is the nature and role of many continuing education departments whose success and survival has depended to some extent on their structural and funding marginality. Nor are the current problems of continuing education departments necessarily going to be shared or supported by the mainstream academic community. In a peculiar sense, they may face similar problems to those of the original CAT units. The obverse side of this is, of course, the opportunity to move continuing and part-time education into the main body of university life at a time when the environment for students is changing and where the need for more flexible forms of study will become the norm. With credit as their tool they will face many of the same threats and opportunities experienced by credit practitioners in the late 1980s. It is an irony that, as was noted earlier, many of those early practitioners within the then polytechnics came themselves from continuing education backgrounds.

INTRODUCING CHANGE

Self-interest and survival

Much of the debate, and many of the concerns, about the introduction of modularity and credit are to do with the changing distribution of power and ownership within an institution. Some of these concerns are undoubtedly legitimate. Indeed, if one is honest, they are, for senior managers at least, a desired outcome of the changes being proposed. But it is also the case that many of the perceived threats come about, not from modularity and credit *per se*, but from the broader changes associated with the move to a mass higher education system.

The managerial problem lies in persuading staff that change towards credit can also be advantageous to them and their students, rather than, as many have suspected, simply to the managers. Some staff will actually see modularity and credit as having distinct advantages: many support a more negotiable programme for students; are happy to see alternative administrative structures that free their time for teaching and research; and welcome certain economies of scale that enable them to cope with significantly higher student–staff ratios than current structures are designed to support. Similarly, some staff can see how credit can move them into areas of activity from which they or their students would otherwise be excluded. Interdisciplinarity, for example in areas such as environmental or health studies, becomes more possible, as does the promotion of generic subjects such as languages, business studies or information technology. In-house accreditation is another area where not only has a new market opened up but working relationships that can be satisfying are also developed. The managerial assumption is often that such people are few and far between. This is probably not true. They are likely, however, to be a minority and the issue is how potentially enthusiastic and supportive staff can be placed in situations where their views can be used to effect change. There are normally sufficient niches within an institution for managers to seek a critical, if not homogeneous, mass of individuals willing to support the changes.

More cynically, staff will come on board if they can clearly see survival as the outcome of such a change. The combination of a competitive, target-based, funding methodology with considerable shortages of students in certain subjects and an increased emphasis on part-time recruitment, has allowed some institutions to play this card in order to establish the need and gain more support for more flexibility and choice. It would be a foolish manager who publicly told academics that their job depended on such change, but in certain circumstances, staff are able to calculate it for themselves.

It is interesting to note, however, how rarely these tactics of persuasion and targeting of possible allies are thought out by institutional managers. Too often the view is that either no one will, or everyone should, be committed to the new changes. The political nature of the process and the translating, negotiating and mediating skills required to succeed are often neglected or avoided. The notion that there is a 'critical mass' of committed staff (and probably only a substantial minority) needed to ensure success is not always understood and does not inform the implementation process.

Ironically, given the belief of the ex-polytechnics that they have been at the forefront of change, it has sometimes been even more difficult for their staff to accept the perceived transfer of power brought on by moves towards credit and modularity. This is principally because of the strength with which they hold to the notion of the coherent and progressive course, a feature of 20 years or more of CNAA quality assurance procedures. Many academics have developed a strong identification with the courses and the cohort of students on it. The notion of 'my' students, 'my' course, 'my' cohort, makes the breaking down of these barriers a particularly sensitive issue. Similarly, a strong relationship between the course and the subject has developed. Although modular programmes have been developed at 'course' level – the humanities is a good example of an area which has been developed in this way within many institutions including my own – there is sometimes still a strong link and overlap between courses, students and staff. From such a viewpoint the whole of the degree was greater than the sum of the parts, but often only in a way that could be defined and understood by the academics themselves. This sense of ownership is very powerful, and one I experienced as a course director in the mid-1980s. But it has to be asked whether the sheer volume of students (for some courses, a tripling in numbers over a period of ten years) would not inevitably have led to a change in that relationship to students irrespective of the introduction of credit-based systems.

The Trojan horse

It is frequently the case that change from the top will be resisted simply because it is from the top, even if there are obvious benefits to those involved. One of the advantages of many of the early CAT coordinators was that they were not evidently senior managers. Many had the credibility of academic backgrounds, extensive and recent teaching experience, and a salary not too dissimilar from the people they were trying to persuade. It was also the case that staff development activities to support such developments were much more effective if carried out by academic staff who were already converted and involved, rather than by managers *per se*. An apparent hands-off position on the part of the senior managers of an institution – except when crisis occurred – could be strongly advantageous to CAT practitioners.

As we have already seen, a common practice in the late 1980s was to set up a CAT unit, usually with a small number of staff, frequently with externally obtained or top-sliced funding. While one of the functions was to attract so-called CAT students and set up the institutional mechanisms for dealing with them, such units were also given change-agent roles: promoting CAT, persuading departments to come on board, providing information and staff development. The staff were often academic staff seconded in, the funding limited and uncertain, and the status unclear. Often personnel involved found themselves and their students marginalized. Priorities for further development were frequently overtaken by the day-to-day operational needs of managing CAT students.

More positively, however, such units provided formal notification of the fact that change was occurring, provided some resource, and could act as a focus for interested and enthusiastic individuals within the institution. In particular, if seen as a short-term vehicle for change, they could create a certain level of momentum within an institution, which might lead to broader change. Possibly helpfully, initially at least, they were quite often seen as separate from broader processes of modularization that might be occurring within an institution simultaneously, but in parallel.

In other institutions, the role for those involved in CAT was more clearly perceived as one of academic development than of student administration. The ubiquitous CAT coordinator could be placed within some other group of staff (for example within an educational development unit), or given a free-ranging role. Their job was not to manage students, but pursue objectives identified by committees or, more commonly, the ubiquitous 'task group'. The role was one of providing appropriate documentation (for example, a validated CAT scheme); persuading and cajoling staff to become involved (the critical mass model); and generally creating the conditions by which credit could become more mainstream as an activity.

Such individuals, again often seconded academic staff, were more likely to be involved with any simultaneous process of modularization. Frequently without real resources or a clear position within the institutional hierarchy, they were very dependent on overt support at senior management level and much more involved with programmes of staff development. As their activities continued, two general possibilities tended to emerge: one track might move them into fairly specific and narrow areas (such as APL); the other into the broader arena of institutional change and, in particular, the introduction of institutionally based modular/credit schemes. The career path, if that be the term, of individuals seconded into these areas of activity is notoriously unpredictable. The odd one might end up as a vice-chancellor, others on the academic scrap-heap. Most would develop new, if sometimes tenuous and marginal, roles within administration or development. All will probably feel that, while it existed, their role in developing credit and modularity was both invaluable and undervalued.

Such models of change come from the 'subversive' end of the managerial spectrum, allowing an institution to move from fairly limited goals and limited resources to a position where further change could take place, hopefully with a broader basis of staff support obtained through the process of consciousness raising and staff development. Whatever the ultimate consequences for either the institution or the individual, many institutions would not have moved as far as they did without these initial seedcorn mechanisms.

From the top

For those institutions wishing to move more quickly, and on a grander scale, particularly in order to create a full modular scheme, such devices would be clearly inadequate. To radically alter an institution within a shorter time-scale requires a clear central initiative; a strong commitment of required (and extensive) resources; a willingness to change formal structures with minimal consultation; and committee-based/manager-based processes of change. This might involve cooption of individuals similar to the CAT coordinator, but who would be more clearly agents of managerial decisions, and who would have both less time and less of a staff developmental role.

Their role would be likely to have a strongly administrative bent, dealing directly with staff, and possibly students, in the operational delivery of the programme. Such individuals, while still requiring the political and social skills of the persuader, face a different challenge. For them there is no escape into new and exciting areas of development, or moving towards a new frontier. Instead, clutching David Watson's (1989) handbook on modularity in hand, they must tread a difficult tightrope between impatient senior managers on the one hand, and reluctant, if not antagonistic, staff on the other.

Systems development

Change of the 'subversive' sort is both unpredictable and time consuming. It also means that certain actions have to be deferred. It remains the case that, having achieved an institution-wide modular/credit scheme, even one with strong elements of devolution, there is a need for some strongly centralized systems – management information systems, timetabling, and admissions for example. If a stealthy approach is taking place, such systems cannot easily be put into place in advance of the change. In contrast, a more hard-line centralized model can take these issues on at an early stage.

Whatever the model, there is always the danger of a gap appearing between the academic development and the systems development aspects of the change process. One or the other may be neglected, in which case the success of the whole system comes under threat. Balancing out these requirements is a delicate task. It can be argued that it is always possible to buy systems, and that they are therefore a subsidiary issue. But a strong academic development programme which genuinely gets staff on board can develop a momentum which can overtake and seriously stretch the systems, to the extent that it can undermine the efforts that have gone into academic and staff development. Flexibility can only be offered with strong administrative support and its lack can quickly bring change into disrepute.

The development of systems themselves is a minefield within the change process. This is nowhere more apparent than in the provision of management information systems. Here, many institutions have had to rely on in-house developments created with inadequate resources, lacking adequate specifications, and always behind schedule. The lack of many established precedents, and the inherent non-portability of many in-house products, has exacerbated the problem, as has the long and possibly forlorn wait for the output of national initiatives. A number of commercial products drifted on to the market in the early 1990s but faced considerable reluctance on the part of potential customers to invest in what remained fairly untested products. The arrival in 1994 of the US firm SCT looking to market its Banner systems, used by about 25 per cent of US institutions, from a UK base is, however, a significant indicator of the level of credit and modularity developments within the UK.

What is clear and common is the fact that, ultimately, the systems must be able to manage the individual student much more directly given that, theoretically, each student could be on a unique programme of study. From the point of view of both academic staff and the institutional managers, the student on the module must, of necessity, become the basic building block for their activities. This is a dramatic conceptual shift for both academics, who still want to see the 'whole' student, and administrators, who are used to managing groups of students on specific courses, and within identifiable cohorts, rather than individuals.

Matrix management

It is within this need to focus on the individual student programme that matrix-type models of academic management become an attractive proposition to managers. A common position emerges that academic staff are responsible for delivering the units, often based in fields/subject groups/departments, while 'someone else' is responsible for managing the longitudinal experience of the student as they move towards an award. This could still be a member of academic staff, perhaps a minimalist version of the course director who was often so central to (and powerful within) the old CNAA course model. On the other hand, it could be an administrative function carried out, as in many old universities, by a registry, or in some new universities by programme managers or their equivalent.

The role of the administrator

A strong element in this, which sometimes causes problems particularly to ex-CNAA academics, is the emerging need to separate out the teaching and administrative functions within the institution. Many academic staff on coherent and progressive courses not only had academic control over what the student studied, but were much more involved in (and had power over) the administration of the 'whole' student and their progression. The strength of this phenomenon, which can create considerable barriers to change, arose, it is sometimes argued, because there were sufficient people in the system willing (or needing) to swap a research career for the student management role. This was reinforced by the fact that in some institutions it became a clear (and possibly the only) route to promotion. But this is also to neglect the very strongly and genuinely held view of many academics that it was the student rather than the components of their experience that was significant, and that it was right and proper for academics to focus on, and have responsibility for, that overall experience.

Why this concern is not always as strong in many traditional universities is a matter of some speculation. Those choosing to be ungenerous will suggest that the emphasis on research in old universities is always to the detriment of attention to the student. An equally inaccurate response to that would be that the students in the old universities, with their strong academic background, did not require such attention. Both views are clearly crude while having some limited truth. In practice it was probably the case that academics in traditional universities saw students in terms of their own subject, narrowly defined in terms of the staff member's own research-based teaching interests. The nature of the 'whole' student, at least in administrative terms, was firmly and rightly the province of the administrator. Traditional universities have normally had higher levels of administrative support in this area to underpin that position. It is interesting to see how some of the new universities are looking more closely at this dual hierarchy model, and are now stressing the need for academics to be exactly that and not well-paid administrators. It is, of course, an issue that the big modular institutions such as Oxford Brookes will have already had to take on board.

The push to centralization

Built into the development of an institution-wide scheme and its attendant matrix management structure, are clear centralizing tendencies which will occur whatever the initial change management process. Such centralization can take place at a policy level, for example through the standardization of academic regulations or structures. Or it can be as a result of administrative necessity, in particular in relation to the question of the management of information. For example, it becomes important as students start moving across faculty or department boundaries that rules about such matters as grading and compensation are agreed. It is for this reason that many institutions have chosen to have a separate combined studies or modular programme, with their own regulations, thus avoiding the painful task of negotiating or enforcing a standard model across the institution.

A similar issue is the requirement to standardize assessment practices so that information about students moving across the system can reach the right spot for the student's overall assessment to be determined. There appears to be an almost inevitable requirement for a formalized two-tier system of examination boards where assessment first takes place at the subject/unit level (with appropriate external examination arrangements), and then at student profile level where there is a mainly bureaucratic process that determines overall classifications. This may not be simply a function of credit-based systems but partially a consequence of large numbers. However, it can be perceived by staff as a bureaucratic (and therefore unnecessary) nightmare. In reality the process reflects the normal processes of assessment that have always gone on. The difference is that it formalizes previously informal processes; and it redistributes responsibilities. For example all staff and all examiners may previously have looked at individual student profiles, whereas the new model may restrict access to that process. This, once again, seems particularly subject to resistance in the old polytechnics.

In terms of the management change, these administrative adjustments can take on a disproportionate significance. Each of them can become a symbol for the ongoing, but often repressed debate, about the underlying changes to higher education and to institutional management. More often than not debates about specific losses of control (over assessment regulations, for example) allow the acting out of tensions relating to much broader and generic concerns about personal and professional control. Ironically, as credit-based systems become more widespread within an institution, it may be academics who demand more consistent or centralized practices (for example in relation to timetabling) as they seek to gain control for themselves and their students. The acknowledgement and management of these tensions relating to power and control are another area where managers (and their staff) often pay insufficient attention, forcing themselves into confrontation and opposition, rather than argument, persuasion and compromise. The need of some managers for cleanliness, tidiness and lack of conflict sometimes exacerbates, rather than neutralizes, what is always bound to be a difficult and untidy exercise.

Conclusion

Whatever the process of change, the development and implementation of credit-based systems will involve a complex, and constantly changing set of factors relating to the achievement of the institution's identified strategic objectives. In particular, it must take note of: the desired endpoint to be achieved; the level of commitment to, and priority given by, the senior management of the institution; the extent of the changes envisaged; the time-scale proposed; current practice within the institution; availability of resources; availability of appropriate personnel and expertise; and staff development needs.

How the process is managed will depend to some extent on an evaluation of these factors and the nature and circumstances of the institution. It will depend principally, however, on the leadership style and management structures of the institution. No one model will be appropriate, but managers need to be aware of the balance they might achieve between managing down, up, and indeed across. Ultimately, whatever the speed of change, the scheme will work only when sufficient individuals take its principles on board. This does not require all, or even most, staff, but a sufficient number of them in the right places to ensure that the structures established are fully utilized to achieve their goals. Such goals need to relate both to the educational advantage of the student and the effective management of the institution. In the middle of this, the necessity to meet the professional and personal needs of the staff must not be lost.

Cultural change is ultimately more important than structural change. Without the former, resistance can develop, which, while masked in the short term by apparent major changes taking place, can eventually build up to a point where the systems developed, however sophisticated or successful in system terms, are unable to deliver. Camouflaged subversion takes place and, in the case of credit-based systems, the rhetoric of choice is heavily constrained by working practices that are limiting. In this sense a university or college is no different from any other organization. The model which will take an institution successfully to its goal requires a careful and constantly shifting dynamic relationship between the academic and the manager, the academic and the administrator, and the academic and the systems. Only if these are managed well will the relationship between the academic and the student be successfully changed.

Chapter 4

The Impact upon Staff and Students

Geoff Layer

INTRODUCTION

The impact of change

Credit-based systems can free both staff and students from the unnecessary rigidity of a narrow curriculum framework. However, like many changes, it is not often perceived that way by those involved. Many staff may feel that their security and place in the organization have been threatened because the barriers in the structures that previously existed have been moved. Staff are used to institutional restructuring, but many reorganizations merely introduce new barriers redefined by the institution. Many credit-based systems actually shift the barriers in order that the student can determine where the barrier falls for their own particular circumstances. Suddenly the infrastructure and 'rules' that staff have come to know and love have gone and staff feel exposed in a system where the 'rules' are new and probably rapidly evolving. At a time of change people often prefer the comfort zone of what they know and are used to compared to the uncertainty of the marshy ground of change.

Students on the other hand are initially bewildered by the responsibility for utilizing the choice they are offered. In many cases the choices made are fairly conservative until the students begin to understand the breadth of choice, at which point the folklore begins to spread. Once the choice becomes informed the students learn to say what they want, and when. In the first few years the students tend to spend time learning the boundaries within which they can move and then gradually push back those barriers. Eventually the explosion of choice follows and the success of institutional change is fully tested.

Choice and control

The fundamental issue which affects the smooth implementation of credit-based systems is the academic debate in respect of how much control should be exercised by staff over student choice. Most of the curriculum structures developed in post-16 education over the years assume that a student will follow a particular route towards a specific qualification. That route is primarily determined by the institution providing the route rather than by the student stating what they would like to study and the institution responding. This is, of course, somewhat ironical given the move towards a recognition of market forces elsewhere in society, which if translated into post-16 education means that the traditional 'supply' model needs to be replaced by a 'demand' model. Although it is recognized within this sector that the majority of its 'clients' are old enough to make decisions about their life, we as educationalists have tried to tell them what is appropriate for them educationally. A major move from control to choice places enormous demand on staff time, commitment and goodwill.

At a time when the commitment and goodwill of staff has been fully tested by the general pace of change, it is noticeable that staff resistance to the curriculum change brought about by credit-based systems is the most entrenched. Over the last five years, post-16 education has seen a massive increase in student numbers; higher staff–student ratios; less personalized contact with students; a decline in the unit of resource; the removal of the binary divide; the incorporation of polytechnics, further education and sixth form colleges; an increase in mature students; incentives to move the curriculum towards training for work; a more managerialist approach from senior managements; and a significant deterioration in industrial relations. All these changes have seen resistance from staff, but all have been grudgingly accepted. However, the curriculum change that results from the introduction of credit-based systems tends to activate much more concerted resistance.

The reason for this concerted resistance may lie in the historical structure of institutions, their curriculum and the rewards package, but the line of argument among the doubters is normally expressed through concerns over the student experience. Many of these concerns are valid in that staff have little experience of supporting students within flexible curriculum models. However, the force of such resistance is often based on the structures staff know and want to keep because they are used to them. It is important therefore to identify the infrastructure issues that staff have concerns over, as well as the student support issues. It is only against this background of understanding what staff, and to a certain extent students, are expected to give up within credit-based systems, that it becomes possible to understand the resistances faced, but also to develop the appropriate strategies to implement the new model.

The issues which disturb staff most when faced with credit and modularity include the nature of the curriculum; their own professional role; the relationship to students; and the administrative structures that are needed to support them. We need first, therefore, to consider how these issues are currently perceived, before establishing how they can be dealt with within a credit-based structure.

Ownership of students

Most institutions are organized in a structure that places staff within subject-based or market-oriented units, commonly known as departments, which then have courses allocated to them or developed within them. These departments tend to take responsibility for the delivery and administration of the course and the subject, as well as associated research and staff development. The balance of these activities will differ significantly both between institutions, and within them. The institution will resource the departments to deliver their activities, with the resources for teaching based normally on a model which is linked in some way to student numbers. The tensions that exist within institutions mean that the staff within these departments will constantly feel the need to defend their position in order to seek greater or stable resources. This defence mechanism normally means that the department needs to be as self-contained as possible and seeks little collaboration from staff in other departments. Consequently, there is a tendency to be possessive over students and this rubs off on the students who associate themselves with the department. The staff feel that they 'own' the student and that the department should take the decision in respect of any curriculum or learning changes. The department also provides a base for students and a structure with which they can identify and have a sense of belonging. Such a factor should never be underestimated as a means of effectively supporting students.

INSTITUTIONAL CHANGE

Course structures

While institutions have always had a range of delivery mechanisms, a central feature of the higher education curriculum has been, and remains, the 'course'. The definition of a course varies significantly but in general relates to a definition by academic staff of the appropriate curriculum to lead to a particular named award. This definition might be tighter or looser depending, for example, on the discipline. Thus courses in science and engineering may have very little choice within them, while arts-based degrees may have always had a much more diffuse definition. The impact of the CNAA, with its emphasis during validation of its degrees on the 'coherence' and 'progression' of a course, means that in many of the ex-polytechnics, definitions of the course are even tighter. The institution may have a curriculum structure into which the course must fit or the structure may be heavily influenced by a professional body or other outside body. This will to some extent constrain the options open to academic staff. Indeed, some academic staff will argue that their professional bodies allow them almost no choice. In general, however, it is a course team, made up of a small team of staff from a single department, that is the driving force behind course development. As a result the tendency will be for the course to become insular as all the support becomes the responsibility of the department.

Coherence

Most courses have been designed, implicitly or explicitly, with specific objectives in mind which are based upon the outcomes of the learning process and the perceived academic coherence of component parts. The coherence of courses and the integration of skills and activities has been a major issue for many course teams, particularly those validated by the CNAA and BTEC. In such cases the coherence is determined and argued for by the course team during the planning and review process. Necessarily, however, it will be influenced by the departmental ownership issue. It is normal for course teams to plan in some detail the students' learning programme because otherwise it begins to unpick the coherence of the course as originally conceived.

Assessment regulations

Many of the new universities developed assessment regulations on a course basis within general guidelines developed by the CNAA. In contrast, the old universities developed general assessment regulations which are often institution-wide and therefore create a level of equity for the students – should they move across an institution's internal boundaries – which does not exist within the regulatory diversity of a course-based system.

In some cases, irrespective of the overall model, courses may have, or choose, to utilize the assessment regulations of the validating or approving body. In many institutions, therefore, there is not any requirement for commonality of rules across the institution. However, once students are allowed to take modules in another subject area the lack of equity in such a process is exposed. Students have a right to be fairly treated and different assessment regulations and practice will lead to students with the same profile being treated differently because they are taught in different parts of the institution. There is a pressing need for all institutions to have their own general and consistent assessment and awards framework wherever possible and for that framework to apply to all students.

Professional and external bodies

Many courses have been designed to gain maximum exemption or recognition from an outside body. It is often the case that this external influence upon the curriculum is seen as providing a more predictable route to employment or further training. Consequently, within the vocational education sector and in times of high unemployment and recession, many students seek a course that is linked in this way. Many of these external bodies are primarily concerned with the knowledge aspect of the learning and less concerned with the process, or with the development of transferable and broader generic skills. Many of these external bodies will approve a course on the basis of the written syllabus alone without any awareness of these broader issues. In many cases student choice is restricted, as meeting the needs of the external body becomes paramount and there develops a tension between curriculum prescription and the desire of institutions to determine their own views on the curriculum. These cases represent a view that students only want to choose that way of achieving professional recognition.

During the development of the course, the course team will have discussed the approach to learning that should be adopted. This will have been revised on the basis of experience and student feedback. Because of the departmental nature of the course team, the staff will know each other and be familiar with each other's approach. They will also receive considerable informal student feedback on the process in the classroom adopted by colleagues. In many cases the course team will have designed an integrated curriculum which builds on each other's work. Consequently, once a student chooses something different as part of their course the teaching style is challenged, as that student is not following the same component parts.

Rewards

Reward structures and packages within education have traditionally favoured three aspects of work within an institution: research; course administration; and consultancy. Once again the balance varies dramatically with old universities traditionally emphasizing the first, and the new universities, until fairly recently, the second.

Where rewards have been attached to administration, such responsibilities may have come to be seen by many staff as the only ladder to promotion. Additionally, it was generally felt that the larger and more successful the course, the more rungs an individual could climb up. It was therefore in the interests of staff to ensure that the course became large; that students did not opt for choices within other courses or departments; and that the course fitted the departmental or line manager's objectives.

Administrative systems

The emphasis on the course has led to a number of administrative support structures being developed based on the demands of the coherent course and the identifiable student cohort. It is not surprising, therefore, that the administrative records and reporting structures, for example, have frequently been organized on a course basis. All the returns and records are concentrated upon the course and its team and not on other broader aspects of the provision. This reinforces the authority of the course and makes the introduction of credit-based systems even more difficult, because they cannot easily fit within that framework.

Similarly, in relation to student support, many course-oriented institutions have tended to operate a two-pronged approach to supporting students. The major thrust of such support comes from the course team itself through personal tutors, year tutors and course tutors. Some courses will have specific curriculum tutors to ensure that certain aspects of the course, such as study skills, which are designed to support students, are delivered by the course team. In addition to the support coming from the course team the students themselves may become a support group. If they form a single cohort within a particular course, they may be together for a good deal of their time, following the same timetable. As a result, they face many of the same issues and will rapidly develop peer group support networks for the majority of the students.

The institution itself will tend to provide central student support services either to provide specific services such as careers advice and medical support, or to deal with the more extreme issues that course teams feel they cannot assist with. This model of student support tends to be reactive and in many cases to wait for the students to come to the service. These services have been traditionally underfunded and consequently can provide little more than the 'blue flashing light' approach.

Quality control and assurance models

Quality assurance is an area of activity that has seen an enormous escalation in activity in recent years. It has become a business in its own right, reflecting broader concerns about the accountability of the public sector. For the old universities in particular, this has required the speedy development of a whole range of activities.

Much of this activity has focused on the production of paper-oriented systems operated at an enormous cost in order that an institution is able to claim that it provides a 'quality service'. Since the creation of national funding councils there have also been a number of attempts to link the quality of the teaching with the funding mechanism. Colleges and universities have invested resources in exploring and reviewing quality systems ranging from BS5750 to Total Quality Management (TQM). However, at the core of all the educational debates concerning quality and how it is measured, the institutions have tended to concentrate upon the delivery of the course as the vehicle to measure quality. As we have identified earlier, emphasis on the course is a major obstacle to the full development of a credit-based system and consequently many quality systems are designed on a basis which is alien to the concept of the flexible credit system. The issues this raises are explored in more detail in Chapter 5.

The experience of quality systems is traditionally very varied. The new universities were, until recently, always accountable to both the CNAA and the HMI, external bodies who both had a view of what constituted quality, and who had the powers to ensure that it was delivered. Many of these institutions therefore developed a very similar approach to quality based on a number of stages in the process of course development. Typically this starts with market research into needs of employers and aspirations of students followed by the planning by a course team, of a course based on the perceptions of the course team, employers and market intelligence. Each course will be developed with its own structure, assessment regulations, ethos and management and the proposal will then be considered by a peer group panel who comment and make various suggestions. Once approved, there will normally be an annual review of the course by the course team, utilizing student feedback and taking into account demand, performance, employability and curriculum issues. Finally, a major review every five or six years will be carried out by the course team who prepare a major review document to be considered by a peer group panel.

The process fits well with standard curriculum planning and evaluation circles and closes the loop in many cases. However, the whole process is concerned with the delivery of a specific course. This system does not enable full consideration to be given to the quality issues that arise with more flexible credit-based programmes.

In further education the approach has traditionally been very different. This has been as a result of the plethora of validating and approval bodies that exist in that sector. It is only in recent years that colleges have begun to develop an institutional approach to quality systems. Approaches have ranged from building on higher education's paper-driven, and in some cases retrospective, style to a more lively action-based strategy. Given the introduction of modularity and – through the Open College Federations – credit, there is a move in the colleges to recognize the needs of the flexible learner in credit-based systems.

However, it is rare that any college or university has actually included an evaluation of student guidance within its quality assurance process. The move towards more flexible learning programmes necessitates the development of informed student choice. This requires the development of guidance provision and ongoing review of their provision.

As institutions move towards the establishment of credit-based systems, a series of issues become apparent to the organization. It becomes necessary to shift staff and systems from those positions I have identified above. The reaction against these changes is in part understandable. Staff have learnt to cope with and eventually commit to the earlier systems. They can see their strengths and weaknesses but in general approve of what they have delivered. It is not simple to persuade them that their overthrow is necessary for survival, and it is particularly difficult to argue that these new models are preferable either for them or for the student. It does not appear to help when proponents of student choice argue, as David Robertson does, that it is necessary to change the 'culture of disciplines' and, through credit, to 'dissolve conventional, intellectual as well as institutional conventions'. As a 1995 *Guardian* article commented, language of this sort, admittedly prone to being taken out of context, is likely to provoke opposition, even if the sentiment is right. (Alderman, 11/4/95).

Some of these issues that need to be confronted can be dealt with relatively easily, while others require considerable time to be spent on developing solutions. Even where solutions are provided, many of the teething problems only tend to reinforce the attitude of those staff who do not welcome the change. The institution is then faced with the difficult choice between pursuing the change irrespective of the attitude of staff, or abandoning the corporate policy.

STUDENTS AND CREDIT

A case-study

Most of the initial problems arise with the student experience and the staff perception of that experience. Because the universities have tended to organize the student support and guidance patterns around a course, they do not have the experience required to support a very different type of experience. Research carried out at Sheffield Hallam University in the late 1980s identified a number of significant concerns raised by students on credit-based programmes. This feedback was openly disseminated nationally across the sector through the 10th Anniversary PACE Lecture by the Principal (Stoddart, 1990) and within the institution through a series of staff development programmes and action plans.

The students reported that they experienced a number of concerns. They felt *isolated* because they were all studying individualized degree programmes that had been negotiated with them. Consequently each programme was unique to the student and there was no apparent peer group or cohort for them to relate to. They also felt that they had been *marginalized* because they were sharing units with other students who had formed their own peer group across a whole course. This meant that the peer group was strong, course-related and led to other students, studying the same subject but not on the same course, being excluded. In addition, staff tended to teach from the perspective of the course of which the unit was a constituent part, rather than seeing the unit as a free-standing entity taken by students following different programmes. This also led to the students on negotiated programmes feeling excluded.

Additionally, they felt themselves to be *ill-informed*, and were often unclear as to what they had to do and by when. As all information within the university was organized on a course basis it had to be extrapolated from course documents to be given to students on individual programmes. In many cases it conflicted with information in a different unit in another course they were taking. An example of this would include the rearrangement of a class based on the need of a course, but where the individual student might not be advised because the information was relayed through the course communication system and not through the unit being studied.

More depressingly, they saw themselves as *unwanted* by staff who resisted the move towards flexibility and insisted on looking after 'their' students first. Some staff gave students the impression that they were an intrusion into the course. Staff on the other hand argued that they, themselves, were in the dark and did not know what they were supposed to do. This attitude was picked up by the students, some of whom suffered as a result. Staff would often argue that they were not sure who was in 'control' of the students and consequently it was not clear to them what the role of the School was. This negative attitude was sensed by a number of the students and was a major focus for discussion among them. Finally, the students felt *lost* in the system because the University's student management and information procedures were based on courses. The student therefore was unsure whether the university's records were accurate, and whether they might be disadvantaged.

These problems arose because the university had opted for a phased approach to change rather than a 'big bang'. This meant that initially the bulk of the university's provision was oriented around courses which it had plenty of experience in developing and managing. The flexibility was initially for a small number of students within a culture alien to student choice and flexibility. This move occurred at the same time as a rapid increase in student numbers which put added pressure on the system. Much of the concern of staff, however, was over the concept of flexibility, not increased numbers, as the former was more apparent and easier to argue with.

As the University began to move towards more flexibility, many of the issues were resolved. Staff who had been antagonistic began to see the benefits of the move and contributed to the solving of many problems. The greatest challenge to managing the change appears to be in the transition period. It is here that resistance is greatest and the teething problems are used to compile arguments against the change. Even if a 'big bang' approach is adapted it can only apply to the first year of courses, and two systems and cultures are required to operate as the students already enrolled on courses will be in the University for another two to three years. Indeed the 'big bang' can be equally dangerous as an approach because the scheme has not been piloted. This is expensive and a source of much confusion. Once the scheme grew in size and became more widely accepted as part of the University, the student experience radically improved. It was reviewed in late 1994 and the review panel spent considerable time with students and came to the following conclusion:

> *The Panel was impressed with the way in which students took personal responsibility to ensure the success of their programme of study, often despite the barriers in their way. Students were committed to the Programme and felt empowered by the structure.*

Undoubtedly this improvement is due to the general acceptance of the programme and the fact that the programme has been an important change agent in terms of both attitude and practice.

WHAT IS REQUIRED TO EASE THE CHANGE?

The process of change must include the objective of implementing the change as smoothly as possible. Given that the ownership of the 'product' is very much vested in the staff, the implementation of change is more volatile than in many other types of organization. It is important therefore that schedules and plans are produced, consulted over, disseminated and regularly received.

In order to implement a credit-based system the following issues need to be addressed. First, staff need to be fully trained and aware of the change. This will be one of the hardest tasks as many staff will not relate to the issues involved until they are faced with particular problems that require solution. Consequently, although the phased approach is drawn out and painful, it has the advantage of enabling involvement of staff in the planning for full implementation as they are faced with the problem in the classroom. It is not sufficient merely to provide general staff development sessions: they need to be focused and regularly revisited.

Second, the college or university needs to recognize that the concept of student choice alone will lead to chaos. The choices made by students need to be *informed.* The student needs to know what options are open to them and what the consequences of making these choices will be. If by exercising choice the student cannot follow a particular career, they need to know the consequences of that decision. For the choice to be fully informed the organization will need to develop an accessible module database which explains to the student: what the module covers; how it is taught; how it is assessed; when it runs; and whether there are co- or prerequisites. This needs to be supported by guidance from staff either in a central role or within a department.

Third, the curriculum structure needs to be designed, agreed and understood. Issues such as size of modules/units, core curriculum, semesters or terms and the concept of coherence need to be debated, agreed and confirmed. These are not easy issues but it is vital that they are not allowed to drift as it will lead to a lack of clarity, uncertainty, and facilitate possible resistance.

Finally, the administrative support from the application stage, through enrolment, student tracking and boards of examiners must be thought through. The issue of student tracking alone will challenge the system. Staff are used to knowing who the students are, what they do and where they are going. The introduction of flexibility means that more information is required on student programmes. It will be difficult to develop a system that can deal with all the issues in tracking unless there has been a pilot. It also requires an attitudinal change in the way information is collected and a heavier obligation placed upon the student to provide information.

In order to ensure that staff are committed to the change they need to have the benefits fully explained. Many will be sceptical and see the issue as really being a resource-saving exercise. It is important to highlight these benefits on a regular basis and it may be useful to ask staff to review progress against the benefits. Once progress is seen, even in the painful years, the resistance dissipates and commitment to the philosophy builds up.

Some of the benefits of the introduction of credit-based systems can be articulated through the impact on staff. These can include *subject development*. Many courses are planned on the basis of discussion, debate and existing practice. The development of student choice enables staff to plan new modules and units that build the subject itself rather than make it fit into a course. In some cases this is a major advantage to subject groups that have had their development restricted. In other cases it enables staff to put on a particular unit/module to test demand and, if the demand is extensive, to develop further from it.

The development of the credit framework and the consequent curriculum flexibility also necessitates greater emphasis on, and acknowledgement of, the *independent learner*. They have to exercise more choice, they must think through their entire curriculum, see how it links together, and evaluate what they are going to use it for. The skills of being an independent learner have to be developed much quicker, but they are the skills that degree courses aim to promote and employers demand. It is no real surprise to me that the Presidents of the Students' Union at Sheffield Hallam University have been Combined Studies students for four consecutive years, despite that programme only representing 3 per cent of the student population. The development of independent learning skills equips the student for that role much earlier in their student career.

Another activity which can be enhanced within credit-based systems is *continuing professional development*. Most universities today are placing greater emphasis on full cost, post-experience programmes. In many cases specific modules and units are prepared, marketed and recruited to. These modules will focus on updating, retraining or a further development function. They will generate income and may well form part of any promotional criteria. Consequently many staff find such programmes attractive. By utilizing a credit framework many of these modules may already exist and can simply be taken down from the shelf. These units can then be accumulated towards an award and become even more attractive.

The *student mix* is also altered within credit-based systems. Many staff recognize the benefits that a broad range of students bring to the educational process. This is often espoused as the advantage of having mature students because they can help the others along. Once staff get over the initial threat that having students from different curriculum backgrounds poses, they realize the benefits of having students discussing matters from a range of perspectives.

As soon as credit frameworks are introduced there is an immediate need for the *curriculum framework* to be described and to include clear explanations for staff and students. This is particularly the case with assessment regulations and procedures where practice will vary across the university. While developing these is initially time-consuming, and often threatening, it can become valuable to staff, particularly new members, and the transparency can come to be thought of as desirable.

For many years universities have paid little attention to the *student support framework*. They have relied upon a traditional model of support being provided on predominantly a course basis. As we have seen earlier, once flexibility is introduced major questions are posed for the support framework which needs to be developed in line with the new demands made. This is a major boon and a completely revised framework for staff as it means that many of the pressures they faced due to increasing student numbers have to be reduced as a result of curriculum flexibility.

HOW DOES THE CREDIT SYSTEM HELP THE STUDENT SUPPORT FRAMEWORK?

At first, in any radical process of change there is uncertainty and the systems will not be fully worked through. As mentioned earlier, staff and students will both expect the support systems they are used to. It is the timing of the introduction of the credit scheme that is crucial in ensuring that student support is addressed. There has been tremendous pressure placed upon the student support system and many institutions are now rethinking their approach. This is particularly the case in further education where the funding model compels colleges to enhance guidance and support through the introduction of outcome related funding. Most colleges now have a client services' function and a more explicit support framework. Gradually universities are beginning to review their provision. If the credit scheme is introduced at a time of such change it will create greater uncertainty but will also demonstrate a commitment to improving the student experience. There is no doubt that a credit scheme needs a different support model. The challenge is how to achieve it.

The prime factors that need to be addressed in developing a student support system are: the guidance needs of the student; induction; the explicit role of the academic; on-course and learning support; personal support; and the role of administrative staff. It is important that these issues are included in any review as they impinge directly on the student experience. While these issues are obviously crucial in a curriculum framework predicated on informed choice, they are also important to a more traditional course-based system as student numbers grow and the unit of resource declines. This is aptly demonstrated by the work of HEQC in beginning to establish quality assurance guidelines for guidance provision in HE. If this is then included in the institutional audit procedures, it will be a very powerful tool to enhance guidance provision.

Guidance needs

Many students entering education today receive guidance from a number of sources including schools, careers services, parents, friends and from higher education itself. Much of this guidance is at a level removed from the educational process itself and may well not be as up to date as it should. If we look at higher education it is clear that many of those giving guidance will be relying on an individual experience of a number of years ago, backed up by what they have read or where visited. That may have been satisfactory when little change was taking place, but in a rapidly evolving credit system there is an urgent need for a change of approach.

There has been a rapid development of guides explaining how to get a place in higher education in what is seen as a very competitive environment. However, much of this has not really addressed credit schemes. Universities tend to produce either amazingly complex information that the majority of staff do not understand, or traditional material that is inappropriate for the new provision. Students need to be prepared for the process of evaluating what they want to do and the best route for such a choice. Schools and colleges have all invested in records of achievement and action planning but this has little real effect on the application to higher education and is rarely addressed other than where specific agreements exist. Students need to know that they have to take more responsibility for their own learning when they enter higher education and be prepared to research choices once they have arrived in the institution as well as when they are applying.

Induction

All institutions have considered the induction needs of students over the years as it is such an important factor in the initial few weeks when a student starts a course. In the majority of cases the numbers starting are so large that the actual mechanics of induction have been left to course teams with institution-wide input being limited to the enrolment and payment of fees process. This may well be effective in discharging the function but it does not really consider the student perspective as it can be so administratively driven. The introduction of a credit-based curriculum means that institutions have to consider what they wish to achieve through induction as there is a need for greater transparency and consistency of approach as students will be taking modules from a number of sources and must be fully prepared for each of their alternatives. The credit system therefore gives the opportunity to revisit induction and to develop educational criteria rather than a heavy reliance on administrative issues.

At Sheffield Hallam we were able to take the opportunity to extend the induction period by starting the academic year two days earlier and using that time as a period of orientation and enrolment. It was recognized that the induction process was not a one-week affair but that it should have a clear educational rationale and contain ingredients that enhanced the level of support in semester one. To achieve this, a general framework of information, skills and knowledge that a student should have was developed, and schools and courses were then asked to ensure that this was put into place. There was therefore a general framework that facilitated each curriculum area to deliver an appropriate induction and at the same time ensure a major element of consistency of approach for the students.

CHANGING PEOPLE

The role of the academic

This is a crucial factor that must be considered when designing a student support system for a credit framework. The role of the academic in supporting students has been a cornerstone of the UK educational system for many years. It contrasts dramatically with what happens in most US universities, where the centralization of student support, particularly in the first two years, is a common feature. In the UK the support system tends to have evolved and to be understood, but it is unusual for it to have been strategically reviewed and reworked. The pressures placed on academic staff have, however, increased tremendously and hence the time they have to support students has subsequently decreased. The introduction of credit schemes places further challenges to their role and therefore it is opportune to review this role and to clarify issues. In recent research into student retention rates that I carried out, it was demonstrated that students will tend to talk to academic staff before anyone else if they are considering leaving the course.

In order to ensure that a deliverable and appropriate framework is in place, the role of the academic needs to be clearly defined to both staff and students. Because of the very different nature of credit schemes, the opportunity is there to identify roles and processes that fit individual interests and specialisms. It is possible to design a creative support framework by preparing 'taught' modules of a skills nature and using one to focus on student support. This means that time and, more importantly, resource is created for that purpose because it is part of the curriculum. The module can then be a core module for that programme, to ensure that all students are covered. Some academic staff may become academic advisers in that they have lead responsibility in an area for student support and guidance and hold surgery sessions for that purpose. This model may not work for all subject areas but it demonstrates the flexibility that can exist.

The role of administrative staff

This is where the major change can be seen to take place. Once programmes become larger and flexibility is maximized, the closeness of the relationship between the student and teacher breaks up as students become more anonymous. At the same time systems will become more bureaucratic and administrative staff will come more to the fore. This requires a major culture change, as for years these staff have been 'protecting' academic staff from students and now they need to change completely and become the students' friend. If programme offices are created which students identify as their base and home, then administrative staff will need to undertake the bulk of that work. They have many advantages in carrying out the role as they are around more than most academic staff, know who to contact to ensure that minor issues are resolved, can resolve many issues to the satisfaction of the student, and can always refer to academic staff where appropriate.

There are clearly many training and development needs that must be met but the administrative staff can provide support that academic staff are unable or do not have time to provide. The challenge is to ensure that the referral mechanism between academic and administrative staff is understood by both. The student clearly receives a better deal, raising issues with people who are there and can respond to them immediately, particularly in respect of basic information.

The role of the student

Semesterization, larger class size, and flexible curricula all pose problems for student integration. The peer support process will break down for these reasons and that can have a major effect on the student experience. Institutions therefore have to consider how to replace this mechanism. The strategies adopted need to recognize the difficulties that students have in meeting, but should also take into account the need for support and feedback. To try to achieve this, schemes have been developed around groups created to discuss issues, together with mentor approaches where 'second year' students meet and support new students. In some instances specific support groups have been created and they become self-managing by the students themselves.

CONCLUSION

As we have seen throughout this chapter the introduction of credit raises major issues for both students and staff. Many of the changes will be met with resistance from both groups for very different reasons. If the change is to happen there must be recognition that the water will be choppy and unpredictable for some time until people learn to sail on it. The process of successful change is based upon learning to navigate the water and realizing that some boats are slower than others and can be blown off course, but also that the faster ones can get ahead of the navigation charts of the day and hit an iceberg.

Chapter 5

Credit and Quality Assurance

Geoff Layer

INTRODUCTION

The context

One of the many arguments put forward by colleagues resistant to the concept of credit-based systems is that they lead to a reduction in quality of academic provision and a lowering of academic standards. This argument is normally predicated on the assumption that the existing, time-honoured, systems used to measure quality and to maintain standards are sufficiently understood by all partners in the education system and that they are necessarily the most appropriate. The challenge for the managers of evolving credit-based systems is to ensure that the procedures adopted are consistent with the objectives of credit and are not simply a fudge between an existing quality assurance system and new needs. Needless to say it is virtually impossible to secure a wholesale change overnight. Hearts and minds have to be won over and staff have to see the benefits of the change, rather than merely conclude that the only outcome is an increase in workload and bureaucracy.

The whole issue of quality – what it means and how it can be measured – has in recent times led to much debate throughout the UK and across all sectors of education. This has been particularly the case within the post-16 environment which at the same time has been undergoing enormous structural change. This debate and change has led to the development of more extensive institutional quality assurance systems, new national watchdogs and a variety of league tables. The debate has tended to focus around the issue of the relationship between institutional autonomy and the need for systems to check whether institutions are operating 'properly'. Very little emphasis throughout this debate has been placed upon the changing nature of post-16 education and the implications this might have for understanding and measuring quality. Indeed the Further Education Unit (FEU) publications elaborating the concept of a national credit framework are virtually silent on the changes required within a quality assurance system, both institutionally and nationally. This chapter seeks to explore the effect of credit systems on existing quality assurance mechanisms; identify any shortcomings; and suggest strategies for ensuring that the important issues are considered.

Traditionally the quality assurance systems adopted within post-16 education have been influenced by a number of factors common to all sectors: the curriculum and structural requirements of validating bodies; the student perspective; the use of external examiners and moderators; the employability of successful students; and the requirements of professional bodies. Many systems and procedures exist to test these, and in many cases, different courses in the same organization will have unique issues that must be taken into account.

Within the further education sector the development of institutional quality assurance systems is a relatively new phenomenon. In many cases individual courses were left to address the issues raised without any institutional structure or framework. Consequently, many of the issues were never effectively resolved. In some curriculum areas it was unusual to have a concept of a fixed course team, given the nature of the courses provided. The focus of any review has always been the actual student performance and not necessarily the educational process and the student experience. A major factor in this approach has undoubtedly been the vast array of courses offered, ranging from very technical advanced courses to mixtures of full and part-time A-levels and increasingly degree-level provision. Given such breadth it is not surprising that there has been no institutional curriculum structure and therefore no college-wide quality assurance process. This situation has, however, necessarily begun to change as the sector has paid greater attention to the development of unitization and modularity.

In contrast, in higher education the concept of peer review, course teams and institution-wide approaches has existed for much longer. Consequently, there has been considerably more time to develop a culture of quality assurance and the need to review progress continuously. As we saw in the previous chapter, the basic approach adopted by many institutions has been one of a course team preparing a course proposal for discussion within a committee or a specifically created approval panel which, once approved, is subject to regular reviews by the course team and students, with external examiners to advise and comment on the assessment process and standards.

Not surprisingly, such approval and review processes are based upon the concept of a specific and relatively self-contained course that the institution is providing or seeking to provide. The process does not address what else is of a complementary or similar nature within the institution. As institutions have moved to the concept of more devolved budgets and tighter control over student numbers, this has inevitably led to an element of internal competition rather than cooperation. It is interesting to consider whether a course is seen as being owned by the department or the institution. The greater the emphasis placed upon ownership of the course by the department, the greater the possibility that curriculum rigidity will set in as avenues outside the department which might strengthen the course are not explored.

Many of the courses developed in higher education are based upon an institutional perception of what the student wants and, increasingly, what is required by the economy. It is essentially a provider-led educational offering. Many of the courses are in high demand in respect of student application rates and have good records for students entering employment. Many staff will argue that because of these good performance indicators we should leave the system alone. This argument is, of course, based upon the concept of a traditional higher education system. It does not take sufficient account of the changes that have taken place and are planned to take place in respect of reductions in the level of student financial support, with the consequent need for students to pay their way through their educational careers.

Once students become 'clients' in this way, then the whole issue around the content, timing and sequence of the curriculum becomes more apparent. This is currently apparent with many part-time students, but will become more common as the increasingly apocryphal 'full-time' students, trying to work their way through college, become more demanding.

While it is true that many students apply for specific courses, it does not necessarily follow that the chosen course is the ideal one for them. The student is merely choosing from the range of courses available, through a procedure that is itself highly circumscribed, and in some cases their ideal course may not be offered, or even exist. In any case, many staff will argue that their particular course development fits what the employers are seeking and therefore has to be organized in this particular way. This possibly self-seeking view is often contradicted by an equally prevalent view that employers do not really know what they are looking for.

Additionally, a professional body may well be involved where a course is seeking exemption or accreditation for its students. Each professional body will approach the task of accreditation in a different way. However, they do develop new policies and practices as the educational debate develops. These bodies are, however, often portrayed by academic staff as dinosaurs who inhibit change and will not allow any meaningful discussion or development. Alternatively, it may be argued that it is more often the case that staff are using the professional body as a smoke-screen to prevent a change that they do not wish to see. So although the course is normally developed and provided to meet student demand and the needs of employers, it is not clear how those needs and the validity of the demand can be measured. It is more likely that the proposed course has arisen from a complex combination of what students may wish, what employers would like, and, to some extent, what staff choose to teach. It is the latter position that is not normally publicly recognized but is acknowledged privately within institutions. It can, of course, be legitimately argued that there is a very strong case for staff teaching the courses they are interested in because the extra commitment which it brings must enhance the quality of the student learning experience.

Institutional issues

In higher education, the Further and Higher Education Act of 1992 radically revised the structure for quality assurance and quality control within the new unified sector. Prior to the legislation, institutions were either given degree-awarding powers by Charter or were 'licensed' by the CNAA or another university. The institutions had developed their own procedures for ensuring quality. In the case of the new universities, this had been done through the guidelines and procedures of the CNAA. Increasingly, though, the government was expressing an overt interest in how quality was assured, and specifically how standards were maintained within higher education, given the major increase in student numbers. In the old universities, lacking the public watchdogs of the CNAA or HMI, this precipitated a move towards a process of academic audit 'owned' by the universities themselves but operating through an independent body on a national basis.

The Further and Higher Education Act introduced a new framework into higher education by concentrating upon both quality audit, where an institution's procedures are examined and assessed by a panel of peers to ensure that quality assurance procedures are in place; and quality assessment, where a particular subject area is visited and the quality of teaching and learning is assessed. The audit role is carried out by the Higher Education Quality Council (HEQC), which is an organization owned by the institutions themselves and based on the previous Academic Audit Unit (AAU) set up by the old universities, although revised and amended to take account of the broader sector. The quality assessment role is carried out by the funding councils and their conclusions can potentially affect the level of resource given to institutions in specific subject areas. Although both processes claim to relate to the individual institutional mission, the diversity in the sector challenges this. A debate has therefore emerged about the effectiveness of both processes. At the time of writing, both have gone through virtually one full round. Both have faced many problems in producing outcomes that satisfy their various constituencies, and assessment in particular has had to make some major adjustments to its methodology. Three years after the 1992 Act, there is a real sense that the balance and scale of quality assurance has yet to be adequately defined. The emergent view from the institutions is that there needs to be one body for the sector. For the purposes of this book, two conclusions are important: first, that the current processes constitute too much quality assurance, possibly at the cost of delivering quality; and, second, that no one has yet seriously tackled directly at national level, the issue of quality assurance in modular or credit-based systems. While the methodology of audit is more sympathetic to flexible programmes, this is principally by default because it simply addresses the institution's own procedures. It does not, therefore, even within its current guidelines, address the issues at a cross-institutional level.

The urgent need for these issues to be tackled was addressed in some detail within the Robertson Report which proposed a range of possible actions including the production by HEQC of guidelines and 'protocols' for all forms of credit-based learning and a number of specific activities that would support institutions, including a national credit register, a credit evaluation service, and a credit compact. However, as Robertson himself pointed out, it is 'clear that no one arrangement guarantees to meet the objectives of quality assurance and easier credit transfer within a framework of institutional academic autonomy' (1994, p.188).

Similarly in further education the HMI function of assessment has been replaced by a concept of audit and assessment. Interestingly in this case both functions are carried out by the funding councils. This is probably due to the fact that no national system of quality assurance existed for further education in the same way that it did for higher education and there was not the same tradition of institutional autonomy. This allowed for a greater degree of central prescription.

Challenges

As the quality assurance frameworks were being revised in both sectors there was a major leap forward generally in the appreciation of the value of quality assurance across the whole range of British industry and the service sector. The Department of Employment initially, and then the Training and Enterprise Councils (TECs), were major catalysts in raising the profile of kitemarking approaches such as BS5750 and Investor in People (IiP), or broader quality initiatives such as Kaizen or Total Quality Management.

The emphasis being placed upon the need to demonstrate quality was growing at a rapid pace. The challenge for education was to fit its evolving systems into a changing external climate at the same time as it was reviewing the organization of its product – the curriculum.

CONCERN FOR QUALITY

But what about credit?

This was the big challenge for credit zealots. They were employed in relatively large organizations serving thousands of students and the organizations had a number of major change items on their agendas. There was a need to determine how to address a range of issues raised by increased flexibility, including: student choice; the crossing of departmental barriers; the recognition of learning gained elsewhere; the tracking of students; student transcripts; the accreditation of in-house training schemes; the promotion of wider participation; and the creation of the independent learner.

At the same time colleges and universities were faced with other major and competing developments which fundamentally affected the organizational structure and its ownership, as well as the funding methodology. Among some of the issues competing for institutional attention were: the incorporation of polytechnics and then colleges; the expansionist funding methodologies which seemed to change every year; the pressure to increase student numbers; changes in research funding methodology; continual changes in the funding and structure of teacher education; the removal of the binary divide; and the abolition of the CNAA.

It is hardly surprising therefore that institutional sceptics could push to the bottom of any agenda issues that tried to address the incorporation of credit issues into the institution. Of course, once the issues were not addressed the same sceptics could easily point to evidence that the credit systems did not work.

Universities were seeking to ensure institutional autonomy at a time when the government was seeking public assurance that the expansion it forced upon the sector had not led to an erosion in standards. There is, of course, no definition of standards but there is an often-expressed claim that they are falling or are likely to. This gut reaction approach can already be seen in the schools sector where improvements in GCSE and A-level grades have been queried on the grounds that either the questioning or the marking must be getting easier.

For many years, the issue of standards in higher education took second place to the need to improve quality. But the unification of the sector appeared to bring out the politicians and the sceptics and before long the issue of the 'gold standard' was once again to the forefront. It was not long before Ministers were starting to ask whether 'a degree was a degree was a degree'.

As with schools, the increasing number of graduates and of students gaining good honours degrees has raised the question: 'Is it getting easier?' Within such a climate it is not surprising that many institutions enhanced the quality assurance of the organization as a means of establishing that the issues were being seen to be addressed. This did not necessarily mean that the quality of the student experience improved but it resulted in copious papers and procedures that raised questions and concerns. The responsibility for resolving issues raised was generally placed on academic staff at the chalk face as part of a movement towards devolution and embedding ownership of the process among all staff.

Staff often saw this as an expansion of the bureaucracy at a time of a declining unit of resource and an increase in their workload. They were often cynical over whether the approach would actually lead to any improvement in the student experience. Consequently it became simply another chore which had to be done. However, this chore has a sting. Course teams feel they have to demonstrate a positive student experience, otherwise their future may be at risk. Therefore they tend to be defensive about the parts they can control, but highly sceptical about other issues that the centre is expected to resolve. In other words, course teams were better able to defend themselves (even if no one was attacking) if they worked within an environment over which they had the most control. The development of credit-based systems challenged their control and therefore created resistance to change.

The major challenge for the management of change was therefore to ensure that the quality issues around credit-based systems were not neglected. As the quality arms of the institutions swung into action there was an understandable tendency to design quality assurance procedures on the basis of the provision everyone knew and loved. The campaigners for credit were left with two stark choices. They could either become involved in the institutional approach and try to change it from within, or they could remain outside the institutional mainstream and bear the risk of losing everything that had been worked for.

The approach adopted depended upon where the credit initiative came from within the institution. In a number of cases the energy and drive was to be found in a Department of Continuing Education or in an area with responsibility for widening participation. Many of these bodies or groups were not necessarily seen as part of the mainstream provision and may not have had any direct involvement with the quality assurance process. This meant that they were unable to ensure that credit issues were encompassed within the overall institutional quality assurance process. In the cases where the credit initiative was housed within a more central department or grouping, then the scheme shapers tended to become part of the quality assurance committee system. They were then able to ensure that credit issues were very much at the centre of the appropriate committee's agenda as it designed and reviewed the quality assurance process.

The key factor in ensuring that quality issues are addressed is therefore the willingness of those who run the institution's quality assurance processes to take on board, as a central feature, the credit-related issues. Because the quality assurance process is founded on a committee cycle and decision making structure, it is imperative to ensure that the committees themselves address the issues. The importance of the quality committee cannot be underestimated as it has enormous influence on the nuts and bolts of curriculum provision and the measurement of progress.

It is interesting to examine the impact of the credit scheme at the University of Northumbria at Newcastle which introduced one of the first credit schemes. This scheme was housed within the Access arm of the university and, although it carried out an enormous range of development tasks, its real effect on the university came when it was able to influence the assessment regulations of the institution. It could only achieve this because it referred issues to the Quality Committee and it had sympathetic colleagues on that committee.

At Sheffield Hallam University the embedding of credit issues was rapidly placed on the agenda of the institution precisely because it incorporated the management of the scheme into the quality assurance framework. We were able to agree procedures for the credit rating of external provision, short courses and the approval of individual student-negotiated programmes within six months of the scheme being validated. The key to this pace of implementation, coupled with constant review and evaluation, was undoubtedly the involvement of our key staff in quality committees and a high level of Registry support at a senior level.

Those institutions that adopted the 'big bang' approach faced a very different challenge as they could not afford the Northumbria or Sheffield Hallam process of gradual change. They were adopting a completely new curriculum framework for all courses and therefore needed not only to revise the quality assurance process but to make it work straight away. Predictably the new curriculum would not meet with universal approval of staff who would therefore seize on any gremlins in the system as irrefutable evidence that the change should not have been made in the first place.

Of course, the big danger in becoming involved in the institutional approach of universities like Northumbria or Sheffield Hallam is that, by definition, it takes time. Much energy is spent arguing for a purpose rather than developing the actual credit-based system. It is a very difficult tension to try to resolve as the understanding of credit is vital to the development of an appropriate quality system. The experience of many institutions is that the only way to change practice and to have the issues recognized is to involve the key people in the debate about the change required.

The biggest problem, though, is the pace of change. Whatever approach is adopted by the institution to introduce credit, or any other curriculum framework, there will have to be a period when at least two quality systems are operational and for a significant period the new system will cater only for a smaller number of students. This is because the old system has to be utilized until the new system is fully in place. Even where the 'big bang' approach has been used it would normally only apply initially to first year students. Having two systems is resource intensive but inevitable, whatever the change is. Many staff will ask if the resource implications of the new system have been costed, though almost certainly they will never have considered the cost of the existing system. Using two systems can lead to confusion but it does allow constant adjustment of the new system to reflect new practice.

Despite the problems, I am convinced that the need is to invest considerable time and effort in the quality assurance process and to ensure that the change is not just cosmetic but can be measured in a realistic and appropriate way.

SPECIFIC ISSUES FOR THE QUALITY SYSTEMS

As explained above, the development of credit has posed a significant number of challenges for the quality assurance systems and here I try to explain the issue in depth and look at strategies that have been adopted to ensure progress. When credit is first introduced it brings with it a new way of viewing the curriculum structure. Staff immediately map the regulations and practices of that framework on to their own course. They see changes that they do not necessarily understand or agree with and complain that this inconsistency is a result of the credit scheme which therefore must be wrong. What is not initially apparent is that this is merely introducing consistency of practice and is in effect highlighting the previously unrecognized lack of consistency and accountability within conventional curriculum planning procedures.

Curriculum transparency

Lawyers can tell you what a law degree looks like; engineers can tell you what an engineering degree looks like; and historians will tell you what a history degree looks like. It is rare, however, to see any transparent definition of a degree that would be understandable to those outside of a particular subject or discipline. Reference is often made to the honours component of a degree but there is no real explanation of the degree itself. For many, the honours degree simply represents three years' full-time study at university after entering from school with A-levels, with the work of each year of the degree requiring greater power of analysis. At the end of those three years, degree level is reached and the debate is then about how good a degree has been awarded.

This system has worked for many years as we relied on colleagues and peer groups to concur or judge that a course was being delivered at degree level. These colleagues were specialists in their field and they would therefore know the standard and level that was required. However, once the curriculum starts to become more flexible and interchangeable, then a whole series of practices come to light that do not fit the definitions and practices of a credit-based system. These practices may well have been appropriate for the particular course they were planned for, but they become questionable when exposed to a broader context and a more mobile clientele.

Assessment regulations and procedures

One of the major issues relates to assessment regulations. Many of the old universities have had institutional assessment regulations for many years and they enable decisions to be taken at course level. The new universities had worked for many years within the CNAA framework, which provided parameters within which individual course teams could draw up their own regulations. This inevitably meant that within either system students at the same university could be assessed for degree-level performance through the use of different regulations or practices. It is quite common for some courses to adopt anonymous marking by using student numbers as opposed to names on essays and exam papers. This makes it very confusing for the student who, in the pressure of the examination room, may enter a number when it should have been a name, and also for the staff member who comes to mark the script and may have no idea what the number means. Similarly, courses may well have very different practices in respect of a range of issues such as late submission of course work, feedback on coursework, or pass marks. Such diversity is manageable within a self-contained course but can create havoc, and ultimately inequity, for both staff and students once mobility becomes the norm.

One of the most common causes for concern is the honours classification system and there is no common system across the sector as a whole as to how to calculate a good honours degree. In some universities each course may well have its own formula: some will use Level 2 credits; some will use all the Level 3 credit; others will only use a percentage of the Level 3 credit. Yet the proportion of good honours graduates is regarded as an important performance indicator for the sector as a whole. This variability factor was not so obvious or acknowledged when students were following traditional degree courses. Once students start to take modules from different courses, and talk to the students on that course, they become aware that their degree classification could change depending upon which regulations are used.

It is not only the students who become critical of the system but the staff as well. They also see inequity, but from a different perspective. They are only aware of the practice they have used and therefore find variances difficult to accept. There is an inherent assumption that their own way is the right way and that these strange students who are taking a negotiated package of modules are getting an easy ride and are challenging the standards of 'their' course. It is only at this stage that it becomes generally accepted that there is a need for common regulations across all courses. There will still be resistance as many staff will argue that they need very specific course regulations and that general university regulations will not have the flexibility they require. This was a major challenge at Sheffield Hallam where institutional regulations were developed that insisted that student performance was measured in credit points, that consistent pass and fail criteria and marks were developed, and that reassessment procedures were standardized. All of these changes were controversial as it meant change to practices and behaviour and it seemed to be the 'tail wagging the dog'. All may have agreed on the need to standardize but they were equally certain that their own model was the one that should be standard.

There was also the need to constantly review the regulations which meant that revisions were introduced each year over a four-year period. With any change of this scale there is always a traumatic period when colleagues are learning together and any problems are immediately regarded as the problem of the change, rather than it being recognized that all the procedures and practices were not really perfect before.

Once the procedures begin to settle down and be understood, they become owned by those using them and are eventually accepted. This whole process takes time and patience to achieve. The drivers of the change need to accept that the system will not become perfect immediately and to accept reasonable amendments, but also to remain dogmatic about the need to make progress.

Student feedback

Increasingly, the market orientation of all public sector institutions means that the definition of quality is seen as directly related to customer satisfaction. The reaction of students to the educational experience they are engaged in is therefore an increasingly crucial component of any quality assurance system as it represents the user's view and has the potential to be a powerful vehicle to influence the quality of provision. However, all too often, the procedures adopted do not enable the students to see the change that they are demanding through their feedback being implemented. There are a number of reasons for this, not least the short period of time the student is engaged in study at that particular level.

Institutions have adopted a number of different approaches over the years to try to ensure that student feedback is effective but all these approaches are challenged by the introduction of credit-based systems as they were normally designed to meet the needs of a course-based system. These more traditional approaches typically involved a range of exercises. A very common one across the sector is the *staff/student meeting*, usually occurring on a termly basis and involving staff and a small group of students discussing each module of the course in that year and how it was going. There are of course the obvious problems of the power imbalance in such a process but it has led to appropriate feedback when successful. In an extension of this, some institutions use the idea of *course representatives* who are students elected by their peers, perhaps through the students' union, to represent their views at appropriate meetings such as a course committee.

To gain more individualized but broad-ranging reaction from students, the *questionnaire* has become an increasingly common device for feedback. These are commonly drawn up for use either at course level or across the institution. They are designed to achieve data and reaction from all the students involved rather than from a smaller group. Once the group considered becomes large or diverse, the questionnaire has to become very general and therefore of doubtful value. As to student response and the nature of the feedback, much also depends upon when the questionnaire is distributed.

All of these approaches are flawed when faced with credit-based systems as they are rooted in a course-based structure. They can be adapted for credit systems by taking the feedback to the level of the module so that it is the module leader who organizes the feedback and acts upon it. If this does not happen, the student from the various courses involved in a particular module may be disenfranchised. However, you are then faced with the complete disaggregation of the student experience as there is no cement to hold the blocks together to enable that broader evaluation of the student experience to take place. Some institutions such as Queen Margaret College in Edinburgh have addressed this issue through the establishment of a compulsory skills unit, which includes a feedback facility to allow an overview of the student experience to be considered. This is possible in a relatively small college but once transferred to a large diverse institution can create many problems, not least the debate over what skills should be included.

This issue is a classic example of the effect of having two systems of curriculum management. The systems that supported courses are seen as having worked because they were dealing with a relatively coherent group, whereas the systems needed for a credit-based scheme are substantially different.

Course reporting

A common feature of most institutions is the collection of a range of statistical data concerning the course and student performance. Systems have been developed to collect and analyse the data appropriate to that institution. In many cases they are designed for a course-based system as that was appropriate when they were originally developed. However, such an approach poses problems for credit systems which require student tracking on an individual basis rather than through a course system. This is one of the major factors in the successful introduction of credit systems, as without an adequate student management system there will be a lack of clarity over which students are taking which modules and there will be a real danger that students can get lost in the system. Staff become disenchanted with the change as they perceive a level of uncertainty and lack of the sort of information that they have become accustomed to receiving.

Performance indicators

The use of performance indicators is generally becoming a feature of accountability. While the debate about the use of such indicators in education has been about the need to avoid crude numerical measures, there is no universal agreement on how to achieve this. There is clearly a need to take into account the mission of the institution in developing a framework of indicators and relating it to the strategic plan. When that comes down to the curriculum level it will be based on the prevalent curriculum structure, that being the norm and staff relate to the structure they are comfortable with.

Therefore when an institution is in a state of transition it has a more difficult task in agreeing the performance indicators. In Sheffield Hallam University, for example, the success of the cohort has always been a crucial indicator for the Quality Committee to measure the health of a course. Such an indicator is a valid measure in a tightly knit course structure but once the student is able to vary the curriculum, to change the pace of study, and to enter at different stages of the course, the use of cohort analysis becomes inappropriate. In the first years of operation of a credit scheme, staff will always use the systems they are comfortable with to compare progress. This means that the students on the credit scheme will always compare unfavourably with those on more conventional courses because the system is designed for the latter. The experience at Sheffield indicates that it takes time to change attitude and tradition. We were six years into the scheme before it was finally accepted that, within a university that had adopted the principles of deferred choice, the high use of course transfer procedures should no longer be regarded as a negative factor. On the contrary, it demonstrated that the objective of the credit scheme based upon the concept of deferred choice was being achieved because it *did* facilitate course transfer.

Prior credit

In most institutions the acceptance of a student's prior credit has always been referred to as 'advanced standing' because a student is entering a later stage of the course. Indeed, even the Open University, which was established on the principles of a credit accumulation scheme, refers to this function as advanced standing and has an office to carry out that function. Advanced standing is effectively the assessment of specific credit against a particular course. It is usually carried out by the relevant course leader who will have built up knowledge and experience of people coming from similar backgrounds. The award of advanced standing takes place within the course and does not permeate elsewhere and therefore there is no shared institutional practice or procedure. The introduction of a credit scheme exposes all the inconsistencies in these arrangements. Staff who have been awarding advanced standing suddenly feel very threatened as they are becoming accountable to a university-wide system.

Such an institutional approach requires a common procedure, clear statements of general credit, limits on the authority of the course leader to award specific credit and regular monitoring and evaluation. This is always seen as taking away ownership from the staff involved at course level and replacing them with more bureaucracy. It is a painful journey until staff start to see the benefits. An example of taking staff along with the concept can be seen through the use of creative curriculum planning. A good example of this approach can be seen in the many 'top up' programmes that now exist. Although they didn't necessarily need credit to develop such routes, the introduction of credit schemes has opened the floodgates in this area.

An example is the 'top up' provision from Higher National Diploma (HND) programmes on to undergraduate degrees. Many universities have for years enabled a small number of students to transfer in this way, usually into the second year. The start of the second year was seen as the appropriate entry point as the HND was not normally seen as being equivalent to two years of a degree. Once a credit scheme is introduced staff can see that the HND is worth more than just the first year, but less than two years. It is relatively easy therefore to design a bridging course between the HND and the beginning of the third year so that students may take an additional 40 to 60 credits between the end of the HND and the following October and then join the final year of the degree. Such a proposal is often viewed very positively by staff as it means rapid expansion without the need to promote the course, and also provides relatively safe community in respect of likely performance at the end of the degree.

There is also of course the concept of the assessment of prior experiential learning (APEL) which has yet to be fully embedded into any university. This process enables an individual to apply for a credit rating on the basis of what they have learned from their experience. The concept is not new. For example, the development of part-time business studies degrees was always based on the assumption that the student brought learning from the workplace with them and that this experience was a valuable part of the assessable learning. The difference with APEL is that it is individualized. One person's learning can be different to another's even if they have very similar experiences. Assessing such learning and awarding credit, rather than just facilitating entry to a course, raised a number of issues. Not surprisingly many staff were wary of such a process. How could they assess it? What were the benchmarks? How do you compare performance? How ultimately do you ensure its quality? This caution is easily demonstrated through the relatively small numbers following such a route. The systems that have been developed for such a process are complex and bureaucratic compared to the old process of interviewing people to see what they could do. It is considerably more scientific and accountable in assessing the level of learning and requires new institutional quality procedures.

CONCLUSION

So what have we learned from the experience? This is an interesting question as it needs to be seen in the context of different practices which, in most cases, are transferable to other institutions and across sectors. The development of credit schemes has taken place at a time when there is increasing interest in quality and standards. Those involved in such debates have had to be won over in order to develop procedures that can be adopted and which can then help to win over the hearts and minds of a broader group of staff. There are many challenges left, not least, for example, how the Funding Councils' Quality Assessment exercises will apply to flexible credit-based schemes. Similarly, how will the moves towards greater devolution within institutions, which create tensions between teaching departments and institutional frameworks, be managed?

There are, however, a number of clear lessons, and it is useful to reflect on them. It is important to recognize the importance of quality, as it is vital to the running of programmes and the maintenance of standards. The quality arm of the institution will produce reports comparing trends over the years and ensure regulation in respect of certain procedures. It is an important agency that cannot be ignored, and if converted to the principles of credit-based systems, has the means to carry out much of the work to ensure that systems and attitudes change. There is therefore a clear need to convert the procedurists to make sure that the questions are asked in the right way and then followed through.

Where a devolved framework is introduced, it is imperative that the framework is itself designed to reflect the needs of the credit scheme and not the idiosyncrasies of various sections. It is useful to approach such devolution from a quality perspective by ensuring that it is the quality review process that asks the teaching departments to explain how they link and support the credit scheme. This then becomes an issue that has to be addressed, but it is not the credit evangelists that are doing the asking. It is the institution asking, and in a very public way.

There is a tendency with the development of new schemes for the centre to develop frameworks and to keep control of that framework. The introduction of credit schemes means a radical revision of quality assurance procedures and it is vital that they are not seen as overly bureaucratic and controlled from the centre. As explained earlier the credit scheme is sensitive. It reveals inconsistencies, challenges previous practice, and demands greater accountability. As soon as the new procedures and principles are understood, the framework needs to be devolved and staff encouraged to use the full range of the flexibility it provides.

It is a clear example of the need of credit practitioners to involve the 'establishment' so as to ensure that the required changes follow. Otherwise there will remain an inexhaustible sequence of barriers that cannot be lifted because, while one system is pushing at the barrier, another is pulling it back to stop progress.

Chapter 6

Credit and External Organizations

Robert Allen

INTRODUCTION

The value of 'off-campus' learning

For those, like myself, who have been involved for a long time in the development of credit and modularity, there is still an odd thrill in hearing a discussion on Woman's Hour on semesters and credits, or in walking into W. H. Smith's, taking the *Antique Collector* off the shelf, and finding reference to the fact that Sotheby's are offering academic credits for their educational courses.

Part of this lies in seeing something that has for a long time been discussed mainly by a fringe group within higher education becoming part of a broader and more public platform. Partly, it is the realization that individual students are now involved in higher education who, without credit, would not otherwise have had that opportunity. A third factor is simply the pleasurable feeling that comes from seeing that, despite the day-to-day grind and disappointments of introducing credit and modularity into often resistant institutions, success is possible.

It is for such reasons, perhaps, that a great deal – more than is apparently justified – has been made of those activities, sometimes known as 'off-campus' learning, that use credit to incorporate learning experiences which take place outside of higher education institutions. These can include the credit-rating of the training programmes of companies, professional bodies, government agencies, voluntary bodies and so on. Additionally, the individual experiences of would-be students can be turned into legitimate, credit-bearing learning. In doing this credit has opened up opportunities that were unimaginable ten years ago.

It is this sense of breaking through, and increasingly breaking down, the long-established walls encasing higher education that can excite the credit practitioner in a way that more comprehensive and substantive changes (such as the development of a modular scheme) cannot. I find it interesting that, in contrast to the image that credit practitioners sometimes present of themselves as progressive and leading-edge practitioners, a group of modular scheme coordinators meet under the touching and deliberately self-deprecating acronym of MUGS (Modular Users Group, South).

However, when working with companies and other external agencies it can seem that credit is genuinely being used for the purposes for which it is designed: to increase access, flexibility and choice. Additionally, there is the sense of relief that can come from working with partners who have sought the practitioner out, and who actually want (and may be prepared to pay for) what is being offered. I have found it personally and professionally very rewarding to see, for example, staff of the Woolwich Building Society walking across the platform of the Royal Festival Hall to gain their University of Greenwich Business Studies degrees knowing that the first 240 credits came from in-house training and professional development programmes, and that even the final stage – a more conventional educational programme – was done principally in the workplace. The fact that this might only involve a few dozen students is forgotten in the moment, because the symbolic impact is so great. In a real sense, this is the very evidence of the slogans 'Lifelong Learning' and 'Learning Without Walls' that have been promoted by various stakeholders in recent years. Though it is now possible to find relatively large numbers of students who might not even attend – in a physical sense – the institution they are 'studying' at, the significance that has become attached to this aspect of credit is disproportionate to the actual number of students it involves.

Employers and education

When the CNAA announced in 1986 that approved employers' in-house training schemes might count towards the award of their qualifications, even they were surprised by the strong and immediate response from over 200, many very large, companies. A vision of transforming the relationship between higher education and employers quickly emerged. A contemporary report from the Council for Industry and Higher Education (1987) argued that employees would develop best, and most relevantly, when what they learnt at college was interwoven with training programmes and experience at work. This was part of a broader objective they wished to promote, namely that:

> *Government, higher education and industry need to become partners in developing a different kind of higher education system to provide for larger numbers, recruit them from a much wider segment of the population, and offer them a diversity of learning methods and opportunities, often work related, at different stages of their lives.* (1987, p.37)

At that time, the debate about the need to make higher education more relevant to the requirements of employers and the national economy was a hot item on the political agenda – the Enterprise in Higher Education initiative was also just around the corner – and government agencies such as the Manpower Services Commission and the PICKUP programme were unusually keen to hand out money for such developments. Some institutions – keen to move into the credit arena, but reluctant or unable to look to mainstream initiatives – found this a helpful and non-threatening starting point. As often happens when change is being introduced into an organization, it can be fairly small pockets of discretionary funding, and small but high profile projects that can form the base for longer-term and more fundamental change.

Precedent and practice

Inevitably, many would-be practitioners in this area looked to the US for guidance on exactly how to go about this process. As always in the process of educational change, it is likely that someone will have already done it, and there should be no need to reinvent the wheel. While North America was clearly the place to seek precedent, procedures and expertise, it did of course reinforce prejudices, particularly among UK academic staff, that credit was the first move on the supposedly downward spiral to a US-type education system.

Everybody seems to have heard about, and laughed at, the McDonald Hamburger University. In fact about 15 per cent of the US's top 100 corporations have a licence to award degrees, many of them up to PhD level. Additionally, about 200 of the major corporations and agencies have made arrangements with universities for the accreditation of their in-house education and training programmes. However, whether you are impressed or horrified by such statistics, it remains a highly marginal element of the US education system, even after a century of credit developments. A CONTACT report of the mid-1980s was forced reluctantly to conclude – with some foresight given that NCVQ was only just coming over the horizon – that this marginality was probably inevitable because of the different objectives of employer-provided training, based as it was on the notion of 'competence' as opposed to the mastery of academic knowledge and skills. The implication was that the best credit could ever do was to put forward notions of equivalence, but never of equality.

Introducing the credit-rating of in-house training into the UK faced one further barrier not normally experienced in the US, namely a perceived distaste of many British employers for spending money on any sort of training, never mind its credit-rating. When talking to managers it is possible to persuade them that credit-based schemes have the advantage of allowing students to study for an award without too much time away from work, as well as enhancing the vocational and organizational relevance of their employee's studies. However, they often have serious concerns, principally that it might unfairly raise employee's expectations (a peculiarly British concern), and also might lead to demands from higher education for more academic approaches to training.

It was against this apparently unpromising background, that a number of very exciting initiatives were to occur. It was much helped by the fact that in the early days of the CNAA's initiative there was sufficient interest among some companies for pilot schemes to be quickly introduced, and some mechanisms and procedures to be developed. In particular, the CNAA and the Manpower Services Commission funded a project, managed at the University of Greenwich, to deliver credit-ratings for a number of in-company training programmes. The companies included IBM, Sainsbury's, the Woolwich Building Society and the Brewers Society. Some of these exercises were to develop into sophisticated partnership arrangements, but their principal success was in rehearsing the particular problems that come from dealing with what was, to most academic institutions, an unknown (and to many, unacceptable) commodity.

METHOD IN THE MADNESS

Assessment of prior experiential learning

Such schemes tested out the boundaries of what people, even the most innovative, could do at that time within the UK higher education system. They made not only academics nervous but also academic standards committees, funding bodies and finance departments, academic registrars, and indeed much of the education community. Where, I have often been asked, is the line between this and giving away degrees? This concern is never greater than when the assessment of prior experiential learning, usually known as APEL, looms into view. However, the ability to give credit to all forms of learning is a central philosophical plank for credit practitioners. In addition, though for somewhat different reasons, there is in the UK an increasing emphasis on the idea of 'competence' and therefore a very strong pressure to devise ways of assessing and valuing experience. Educational ideology, political imperative, and commercial opportunity therefore come into strong juxtaposition. Some people might well consider this an unholy and unhealthy alliance, but it also opens up for others opportunities to break down some of the walls surrounding higher education.

The Learning from Experience Trust has been promoting experiential learning for many years and has had a considerable influence on both this activity and the development of credit generally. Its Director, Norman Evans, wrote in 1988 that APEL had become 'one of the totem phrases concerned with enhancing education and retraining and boosting the economy'. Even he, however, had to admit the awkward nature of the term 'experiential learning' and confessed that it had a 'touchy feely approach to learning which sends shivers down many academic spines'. He had a personal preference for the alternative term 'prior uncertificated learning'. Although now well established in some institutions, APEL probably still causes that reaction in many people. This is not helped by the fact that, even if it were generally considered to be desirable and possible, it is clearly never going to be an easy thing to do. How, asks Norman Evans, can you assess the 'incidental, often unintentional learning lying higgledy-piggledy inside people so that valid judgements can be made'. It therefore remains one of the more difficult, and therefore under-used, elements of the credit framework. But, as with the credit-rating of in-house training, it serves a symbolic purpose in clearly identifying the purpose and potential of credit as a basis for delivering fundamental change. It can act as a banner for those to whom credit is a tool for transforming education, not simply for reorganizing an institution.

Over the last few years, however, a number of steps have been taken to smooth its way. A lot of hard work has been done in reassuring the sector that APEL does not undermine it. It is always emphasized by its supporters that experience, in and of itself, cannot be awarded credit, only the demonstrated learning that results from it. The importance of evidence and learning, together with better developed procedures for determining and evaluating them, have done much to allow an increasing number of individuals to take advantage of the facility. Nowhere is the importance of staff development in changing attitudes so evident. It is particularly interesting to see the response of individuals when they are given the opportunity to assess their own, or their colleague's experiential learning. In practice, most people believe that the experience of their working (and even personal) life is as valuable and therefore creditable – if not more so – than their formal qualifications.

APEL will always remain, as it has in the States, a comparatively small activity. Its significance probably lies more in its ability to demonstrate the principle that learning can take place anywhere and all learning can be credited. Its very extremism can be a useful tool in promoting that point. At the very least, it makes the assessment of prior certificated learning look fairly commonplace.

Measuring credit

In determining a credit-rating of any educational experience, the two principal issues are size and level. Within the normal provision of an educational institution, this is (or should be) a straightforward activity because any 'course', 'unit', or 'module', can be measured as part of the overall student experience, and normally in relation to a set of not always explicit norms or criteria. In-house training, however, is likely to be non-standard, even at the most general level. The evaluators working on the CNAA/MSC project found that printed materials within companies were often difficult to gauge, and their significance might only emerge after detailed discussion with company representatives. Even then, precision was often difficult, particularly as assessment tended to be basic or non-existent as a device for determining the outcomes, and therefore the credits, of a programme. In some cases, evaluators were confronted with genuine experiential learning with no formal study or formal instruction involved.

In that sort of situation, expertise and judgement (often combined, and then unhelpfully disguised as 'intuition') are crucial. Such judgements are, of course, both legitimate and inevitable. This reliance on judgement is sometimes used against proponents of APEL, the unspoken assumption of the critics being that conventional academic life inside educational institutions is always subject to transparent rules of objectivity and rationality. As a result, evaluators of employer-provided and experiential learning are likely to be faced with, or make for themselves, demands for precision that would not be expected elsewhere.

Size

In view of the many variables involved, some informal or *ad hoc* assessment of 'size' is normally the evaluator's first step. Time is the normal starting measure, though there are obvious problems with this and its usage has been another of the major theological-style disputes within the world of credit and modularity. In particular the often heated, inherently parochial, and still unresolved debate within the UK about the utility of the Further Education Unit's 30-hour credit, as opposed to the CNAA's 120 credit/year tariff, is one which has both been influenced by and had some impact on this area of activity. It would undoubtedly be easier for the purpose of credit-rating were there one simple formula, nationally agreed, that related credits directly to learning hours. In practice and as usual, within higher education at least, pragmatism and arithmetical skill are going to have to suffice to resolve this dilemma.

In-house training can be either shorter or much more intensive than comparable activities in educational institutions. The CNAA requirement that anything credit-rated had to be at least four credits in size (equivalent to a week of full-time study inside a higher education institution) reflects concerns about what can justifiably be seen as 'real' higher education. Ironically, those carrying out credit-rating quickly discovered that a week of employer-based training could warrant much more than four credits because of the very intensive nature of the experience. But the act of credit-rating forced both university and company-based staff to acknowledge their different practices and to seek what was common. More often than not, there was much more than was anticipated.

Such activities therefore exposed and confronted some of the assumptions underpinning higher education. For example, on the CNAA/MSC project, one of the evaluators started off with a formula that took one credit point per day of study as a starting point. Thus, it was argued, the 120 credit points needed for one year of a degree, could be obtained by 120 days of training, at seven hours a day, that is about 840 hours of study a year. This was felt, taking practical activity into account, to be roughly comparable with the weekly workload of an undergraduate with a curriculum of 20 hours/week. Such a formula is quite neat but the evaluator commented, significantly, that 'while attractive in its simplicity, this formula in practice tended to undervalue some of the courses when compared with their *intuitive worth*'. A refinement was therefore developed which came up with what was seen as a more 'realistic' judgement of 1.4 credits a day. Thus some of the assumptions of the worth of external education were quickly undermined and the case study was to provide both a precedent and an exemplar for others who went on to work with other companies and agencies.

In the US, the first accreditation agencies worked out the standards through experiment and experience. As more experience was accumulated, more standardization was built-in based on the knowledge of what had gone before. In practice, it was found that assessors, both academic and non-academic, came up with similar answers, whether they were new or experienced. A similar experience seems to have occurred within the UK over the last few years, and there are now a relatively large number of people who have been able to carry out such activities and have shared their experiences. It remains to be seen whether the standardization that is achieved is only internal to specific institutions, or whether there is an emerging national consistency. This remains a matter of considerable debate, even among experienced credit practitioners, but the ever broadening use of external people by the CNAA, the Open University Validation Services and individual institutions provides an opportunity for a wider consensus to emerge.

Level

Having come to some agreement about size, evaluators are then faced with a possibly even greater problem, that of the academic level of the learning that has been undertaken. Even within educational institutions, where it is assumed that such distinctions between levels are both clear and generally agreed, the question of level, and particularly the distinction between postgraduate and undergraduate level, remains problematic. Credit and modularity often expose (and are sometimes blamed for) these differences. Given the lack of highly specific criteria relating to level, evaluators of external learning often find assessment very difficult, particularly if their only experience is within academic courses. Indeed the early judgements on in-house programmes often emphasized 'limited academic inputs', 'the need for more theory', 'lack of breadth', and the lack of conceptual problems. As a result, credit-rating events have become notorious for reducing the recommended level of an activity, while supporting the quantitative definition of credit.

Problems of size and level can sometimes be dealt with through negotiation with company representatives; by 'bulking' or 'enhancing' courses; by reassessing the objectives or outcomes; or by broadening the syllabuses. If the assumption is that expertise and negotiation, rather than arithmetic precision, should be the foundation of such exercises, the calculations need not be as problematic as imagined or presented.

Assessment

The assessment of student learning is a standard and perpetual problem in relation to such activities. Many training programmes have no formal assessment methodology, except in the assumed or measured (through appraisal) enhancement of individual performance of the employee in the workplace. However, it is always a prerequisite of the award of credit that some assessment has taken place. This can create a dilemma for those trainers who believe that assessment can destroy the character of what had, up to that point, been a perfectly acceptable programme for both the employee and the company. Indeed, this is an argument used more recently by academics within the field of continuing education generally, and has been one of their central concerns as they have been forced to move into a credit-based and credit-funded framework.

Establishing credibility

It is worth looking in some detail at the activity of credit rating because, although all of these problems can be seen to have practical, and by now proven, solutions, they also present a series of broader issues about the nature of the relationship between education and training; theory and practice; academic and professional. Indeed the very idea that such credit-rating can be carried out was, and still is, treated with some scorn. The fact that the in-house facilities of many employers were often resourced at a much higher level was either not known or ignored. Early schemes such as the IBM/Portsmouth University partnership, or the University of Greenwich/Woolwich Building Society degree were seen by antagonists as 'Mickey Mouse' operations that threatened 'standards'. It was to take a number of years, and external examiners' positive reports, to lay some of these prejudices aside.

To the credit practitioner, the advantage of such activities was that they could be carried out with the involvement of a relatively small number of (probably enthusiastic) people with external funding either from government agencies or the companies themselves. As such, these activities were often an opportunity to practice, and in some situations invent, the principles, and to develop expertise and procedures. It would, in some cases, be the basis for grander developments within the institution.

Companies which became involved saw potential advantages in terms of increasing employee motivation; the elevation of the status of training within a company; the quantification of the value of a trained workforce; the development of the quality assurance of training programmes; and as a marketing device that would provide external validity of the quality of their courses. More cynically, one training manager of a large company commented that accreditation would prove to his directors how good his training was, and that it would help in his promotion. A less typical but more astute comment came, not unexpectedly, from a US company manager who said: 'The legitimacy which college credit offers is thought to be more important to individuals as a motivator than any belief that the training so accredited will have greater dollar value on the external labour market.'

This is not, of course, corporate philanthropy. It attempts to take advantage of the motivational effects of continuing education, particularly in situations where perhaps there is high mobility and problems of recruitment.

THREE CASE STUDIES

Case Study 1: An early employer-based scheme

In the first half of 1987, the CNAA formulated an agreement with IBM for the approval of credits for their in-house training. These could then be topped up, particularly at nearby Portsmouth University. From September 1987 the employees studying the IBM Information Systems School's courses at the company's New Place Centre near Fareham were able to gain credits for up to one year's work, potentially shortening the period necessary for graduation by roughly one-third. Though the link with Portsmouth was initially only one means by which the credits could be cashed in, the relationship was seen as a convenient local opportunity for specialized study.

The scheme was taken one stage further when a group of about 20 students on three-year contracts with IBM started what was effectively a four-year BSc sandwich degree in computing. Working a 48-week year, they combined Portsmouth University and IBM course units, with a number of personal skills/business units being done at the IBM Education Centre. Another unusual aspect was the six-week summer school at the end of the second year. Using this intensive programme it was calculated that the students would complete the normal degree while achieving twice the industrial training.

On the surface then, this was a very intensive version of what some of the earlier pilot projects had envisaged, with IBM's courses being externally evaluated and accredited. Much of the early work was done within the CNAA/MSC project and in their proposals the evaluators decided to adopt the broad approach of 1.4 credits per day for general courses, 1.0 credits/day for IBM-specific courses of academic value, and 0.5 credits/day for supporting exercise time.

But the scheme was clearly much more than the accreditation of IBM units, and its existence and significance lay in other issues. In one sense it was not much more than the old education system customized for IBM. The credit evaluation made the customization easier and provided a legitimizing vehicle for its validation. As such, it was intended – for both IBM and the recruits (usually high-flying school-leavers) – to be an improvement on the existing degree model. It also aimed to further bridge the gap between academic mastery and job competence. It was an early example of partnership, with credit the enabling device. In its use of credit it was both imaginative and limiting, for it pointed to the fact that credit was most likely to be effectively mobilized in the workplace where organizations have clear goals and expectations, from which point they can utilize educational institutions and their credit schemes in a way that suits them.

The area of in-house training and accreditation demonstrates the enabling nature of credit – the fact that it is a tool – very clearly. Most of the programmes built up around it rarely mention credit, except in passing. There are no CAT banners flying, and many of the ideas that give rise to such controversy within the mainstream of higher education institutions are taken for granted and seen as unproblematic. Many of the emergent partnership arrangements could, in theory, have been developed without the existence of the CNAA CAT model and its tariff. But this is to ignore the fact that it was just such schemes that gave the concept of credit considerable profile, while simultaneously allowing both the exploration of relationships that might otherwise be seen as highly problematic, and the creation of a framework within which credit could be applied to a broader range of activities.

Case Study 2: Institutional change

Pragmatism

The University of Greenwich can perhaps provide a more extended case study of how this process can work. As has been mentioned earlier, the university had been one of the first institutions to introduce an institutional CAT scheme which was validated in 1988. Looking at that validation document, it is possible to see that all the required elements for running a CAT scheme are there. It is also clear that the authors, including myself, took a fairly pragmatic position and virtually hijacked the recently introduced CNAA CAT regulations *in toto*. An auditor going into the institution in the mid-1990s might wonder what had happened subsequently to this original scheme, which was reviewed in 1990. They would probably ask how many students went through the scheme. The answer they would get would be that it was less than a dozen.

The fact is that the original document was devised to support a number of initiatives working in parallel, which were more concerned with promoting professional development than individual student flexibility within the university's conventional academic programme. Subsequent to the MSC/CNAA report the university had continued to work with a number of partner organizations, principally developing a degree for the Woolwich Building Society, a Certificate in Higher Education for Sainsbury's, and a Masters programme for the Brewers Society. These were centrally organized under the aegis of a Dean of Continuing Education. The underlying reasons for this approach were both practical and philosophical. The institution had a clear mission to become more accessible but, as well as wishing to open itself more to the conventional educationally underprivileged groups, had identified those already in work requiring professional development as another group with relatively restricted access to conventional university courses. More significantly in the short term, there was money from both government agencies and the partner organizations themselves to support the initial upfront costs of setting up the appropriate procedures and mechanisms, as well as – and this was a crucial element – a programme of staff development. It was also the case that introducing credit in this way only required a small number of committed and active supporters. It could take place on the fringe of the normal educational provision without, in the short term at least, threatening the wider academic community.

Promotion

The subsequent permeation of the credit system throughout the institution was regarded as necessary, but it was clear that if broader developments were to take place, academic staff would need to become more directly involved and to feel ownership. This happened unexpectedly and fortuitously when staff on the University's INSET programme were faced with a major problem that appeared to threaten their survival. National funding changes for INSET provision made the full-time sabbatical for school teachers virtually impossible. There was a need to provide more flexible opportunities within higher education, but also to take into account the extensive provision that was offered within local authorities. Credit seemed to provide a solution to both these issues, and the INSET staff, using the regulatory framework provided by the CNAA, validated an INSET framework that ran through to Masters level, and which specifically made a strong feature of APL and the accreditation of in-house INSET provision. It began to create a model of rules and procedures that were later to become the basis for the development of institution-wide provision.

The significance of this move was that it strengthened the emphasis on continuing professional development as the most attractive market for the use of credit; provided a ready-built model for others to emulate (forgoing the need to reinvent the wheel); and more importantly showed that credit could work. It became particularly attractive when, because of the flexibility of its Masters programme, the Faculty of Education was able to move in only two years from having very few postgraduate students to registering nearly 200. This was of interest to other faculties who wanted, or needed, to expand postgraduate and post-experience provision. But at this stage the introduction of credit was not compulsory. The institution initially allowed faculties the choice of whether and when to take the idea up, and also the freedom to use the structure to meet their specific needs or those of their component disciplines. In this way some sense of ownership on the part of the academic staff could, it was hoped, be cultivated. Thus, for example, the Business School saw opportunities to develop the Woolwich Building Society programme, as well as the INSET model, to focus on partnership arrangements with organizations in both the commercial and the public sector.

Development

Such changes began to involve a broader group of people, particularly through validation and staff development events. It enabled the institution to rehearse some of the problems, for example in relation to quality assurance and funding, and so to create good practice as well as expanding expertise. The model became increasingly portable, and it was evident that the best people to move it around were those who had already operationalized it themselves. The notion of horizontal development, using academic staff to promote central initiatives, was pursued. The then director, a long-time proponent of both credit and modularity, was able to take an apparent back seat, not overtly promoting it, except at crucial moments. Indeed, he quite deliberately seconded me to lead the developments, working on the theory perhaps that my closeness to the academic arena, together with my experience as a course director, as well as a NATFHE branch official, would open doors and reduce resistance.

The university, by emphasizing the professional development aspect of its credit system, was able to use its PICKUP funding to support developments both in the centre and in the faculties, working on the principle that this would allow it to incorporate PICKUP-style activity into its award-bearing structures, hopefully enhancing their marketability.

In this way the university, using a fairly small group of committed individuals, and concentrating on limited and clearly delineated projects, created the structures, procedures and practitioners that could eventually support wider developments. Success stories were used to increase the profile and to gain further interest.

Institutionalization

Like many so-called strategic developments, this institutional biography has a retrospective coherence that was not obvious to most people, including me, at the time. The story that has been unfolding here led eventually to a position in which, by 1994, the university had an established institution-wide, unitized credit scheme at both undergraduate and post-graduate levels. It would be easy to see this conclusion as the achievement of the original goal and all the intermediate steps as part of a planned progression. Even if that had been the vision lurking in the back of the mind of the director, it is probable that he would have been too astute to promote publicly, at least in the early days, such a radical picture of the future. Indeed he had tried to do exactly that in the early 1980s and signally failed to bring the institution on board. Similarly, although he may have held that view, the key players brought in to implement it either did not share it, or held only a partial, and sometimes parochial, view of what was involved.

As an example of this attitude, in these very early days of credit developments, modularity was very much a back-burner issue. Indeed, the strongest proponents of CAT saw it as a quite separate and potentially distracting issue. What they perceived enthusiastically as the astounding, invigorating and ideological features of CAT tended to overwhelm the fact that modularity – rather more dull and mundane – is another very helpful tool. If nothing else, it makes institutions easier to manage and administer. To the purist CAT practitioner at this stage, however, modularity appeared actually to take away from student power, being easier for managers and academics to appropriate and subvert.

As a result, the university tackled the issue of unitization in a parallel, though not completely separate, manner. There was some overlap in the principal players, including myself, but unitization was quite specifically directed at the undergraduate curriculum, and a general reorganization of the academic structure. As has often happened, semesters were brought in on the back of the process. A specific decision was made that the new academic structure would not be centrally managed and it was agreed that faculties would introduce the university's unit structure as their provision came up for the normal process of validation and review. Theoretically, this would take five years, much too long for some, but it reinforced the principle that at least some of the staff needed to feel that they were partly in control of the process, and had some ability to influence the outcomes. Correctly, the university fudged a number of issues: standardization of units; timescale; combined studies. But unitization and, particularly semesters, could not so easily be left to the partial market force model that had been used to introduce credit. It required a much clearer central control. A number of courses moved into the system during the first two years, but eventually faculties moved *en masse* such that within three years all provision was unitized within a common academic framework.

Fundamental change?

The interesting issue for the change manager here is the relationship between the introduction of credit as a vehicle for professional development and the broader institution-wide process of unitization. A clue lies in looking at the academic framework that has emerged at the University. It bears a strong resemblance to the original CAT scheme, the INSET scheme, and the CNAA CAT regulations. It has been expanded and customized, but the essential elements remain. Facilities such as APL may still be under-utilized at undergraduate level, but all provision adheres to an academic framework that emphasizes flexibility and, should people wish to take advantage of it, maximizes the opportunities to move across boundaries and innovate. It is this sense of creating at an institutional level a framework – principles, structures, rules, procedures – that does not constrain change, and makes the process of implementing change quicker and less traumatic, that is significant.

Ironically, the initial separation of the two themes – CAT and unitization – may have enhanced the ability to deliver both of them. Neither got confused with the other. The proponents and opponents of each were separated out. It was possible to defend one, while attacking the other. Eventually, they became apparently as one, but in individual parts of the institution the focus and emphasis can be quite different depending on history or disciplinary need. Both credit and unitization – separately and jointly – have become tools for change that provide both institutional consistency, as well as some autonomy for different disciplinary areas.

Realism

The value of a such a case study is not so much in presenting a model for change, but in identifying elements of that process. The first point that needs to be made is that, as always, change is inherently difficult: there is no easy and tidy way. Management theorists stress the excitement of change management, and that is sometimes undoubtedly there. But in general, it is a murky and problematic process in which good fortune and political skills play as much role as strategy and planning. While the original proponents of the University of Greenwich scheme may end up feeling quite pleased with themselves, this does not mean that there have not been, or continue to be, problems and resistance. Support, and therefore performance, is patchy. Incompatibilities developed in the system and regulatory sticking-plaster became necessary. The emphasis on academic development ignored appropriate systems development until a point at which the overall viability of the scheme was threatened. A stronger sense of central intervention now pervades, with elements of the scheme being tidied up by dictat rather than development. This is partly made easier by an increasing demand from academic staff that, if they must have a unitized credit structure, the university must take more action to support it in a consistent, institution-wide, manner.

Conclusion

It is possible with hindsight to trace how the early credit-based innovations relating to professional development have influenced and underpinned subsequent development. The structures that were set up to manage the early schemes have become the structures by which the university is managed, or at the very least have provided solutions for the problems that arose as the university moved to an institution-wide scheme. Seven years later the footprints of the early schemes, and their proponents, are to be found throughout the university. It may well be that it was their very marginality that served to ameliorate the tensions and stresses of radically reorganizing the institution by providing space to play and practice.

Case Study 3: Back to the beginning

The link between these early innovations relating to in-house training and subsequent institutional change are not, however, inevitable. It is very interesting, and perhaps salutary, to return to that other pioneer of the links between employers and credit, the University of Portsmouth. A newcomer to credit in the mid-1990s, would once again find Portsmouth attracting considerable interest in this area. The focus now, however, is their much applauded and publicized Partnership Programme which started as an Employment Department project in 1991. It is not a company-specific programme, and is designed to enable individuals to learn while still at work, by enabling them to put together a package of work-based learning projects, units of study from the university's portfolio, and the assessment of their prior learning. The publicity for the programme never mentions credit at all, but it is clear that credit is central to providing the capacity to individualize the student packages. Credit is only one of the innovative ideas underpinning such projects – work-based learning, learning contracts, and transferable skills are all features that are stressed – but credit acts as the element that ties it all together.

A 1993 Employment Department report throws some interesting light on the broader institutional issues. It comments that: 'New methods of assessment such as using APL to decide entry point, and allowing students much more freedom to design their own course were all new concepts to University staff.'

The report also admits that, though there was enthusiastic support, some staff regarded certain elements with suspicion, and a few even thought it might lower the university standards. This had led to a significant staff development campaign on the back of the project. In this sense, the project looks like the classic 'Trojan horse' model of change. Although it has only had a small number of students, the scheme begins to introduce staff in a number of disciplines (in this case principally engineering and business) not only to the technology of credit, but to a set of attitudes that opens up the university to previously excluded groups (in this case the full-time employed) by allowing considerable flexibility in determining what makes up a legitimate programme of study.

However, to observers, and presumably some within the University, this necessarily creates a sense of *déjà vu*. What has happened since the introduction of the IBM scheme in 1986? The answer, presumably, is a simple one. The IBM scheme was exactly what it claimed to be: a way of developing a link with IBM. It was not perceived as an element in a broader strategy, or the basis for the development of a new market. It was a tool to achieve a specific, limited objective, not one for trying to achieve fundamental change. It was not perceived as part of the institution's mission, at that time, to pursue the broader objectives that could have been built on the introduction of credit. In crude terms, credit was not necessary.

However, in a new climate, where the possibility of a national credit framework, and with modularity potentially a near-universal feature of higher education, the wheel may well have turned full circle. The Partnership Programme may now serve the purpose of supporting and promoting wider developments and, as with some of its predecessors, have an effect that is quite disproportionate to the number of people actually on it. Supporters can be developed who are able to use their academic credibility to promote the ideas and begin to develop the critical mass necessary to change the overall system. The programme itself, which possibly deliberately underplays the credit element, and is not directly linked to the threatening CAT movement, and in any case doesn't have a major impact on most people's day-to-day lives, can introduce the ideas, attitudes and technology in a fairly subversive way. With what now appears to be strong strategic support from the top of the institution, and an academic development unit designed to support it, the impact of such a scheme on the institutional culture can be significantly different.

FUTURE DEVELOPMENTS

New possibilities

In reality, the uses of credit as a tool to develop links with employers, rather than as a base for broader strategic developments, will always be marginal, though it is now possible to have hundreds, if not thousands, of people taking advantage of such opportunities. But such schemes do show conclusively that higher education can break down barriers, make partnership with employers a genuine possibility, and generally introduce credit as a means by which people can continue education wherever and whenever they choose. In doing so, some of the rhetoric of lifelong learning begins to become practice rather than theory.

There are now a number of major companies that have devised flexible and customized programmes in cooperation with higher education institutions. Some universities, such as Wolverhampton, Anglia, Greenwich and Sheffield Hallam have developed distinct and expanding new markets on the back of these developments. At a time when the search for alternative funding sources has become even more crucial, these are perceived to be a critical source of income generation with, so far, limited sector competition. The demand from employers and employees for increasing flexibility in the provision of post-graduate and post-experience training makes credit a vital and competitive tool. With the battle for decreasing sources of conventional teaching and research funding hotting up, some institutions have perceived a market niche that credit can help them exploit.

Professions and partnerships

Nor is it simply employers who are providing new opportunities. Some professional bodies, notably in the health arena, have seen credit as a vehicle for developing Continuing Professional Development (CPD). As many professions establish CPD as compulsory for their members, they seek more imaginative and flexible ways of ensuring that such CPD is appropriate and credible. The Construction Industry Council, for example, has initiated the setting up of a national credit-rating agency by a consortium of four universities: Westminster, West of England, Nottingham Trent and Greenwich. This provides the mechanism by which individual professionals, as well as CPD providers of different sorts, can gain kitemarked credit for their work. This can then be used as a base for moving on to a conventional academic award.

Other professional bodies such as the Chartered Institute of Bankers have sought to ensure that their professional awards have a credit-rating that will give their students advanced standing at a range of institutions within the UK. Similarly, many local authorities have sought to maximize their training, despite financial constraints, by looking to credit-based partnerships which can deliver, possibly in-house or by open learning, academic awards.

Nor is it simply large employers and agencies. Some small providers of CPD see credit-rating as a means of establishing the credibility of their provision and thus opening up further opportunities and new markets. Recent examples with which I have been involved have included the Lantern Trust, a provider of HIV/AIDS training programmes, and the Age Exchange Theatre Reminiscence Theatre Company which, with European and industry support, provides training programmes for the health sector. In these ways, a range of organizations, in both public and private sector, have started to explore the ways in which credit might be of use to them and their employees.

Providers of services

An interesting spin-off from this sort of work is the realization that higher education providers don't only deliver education and training programmes. What are important to some of the partners are the awards and the quality assurance framework. As such, universities are in a position to provide a specific service. Thus the University of Greenwich, in partnership with the Chartered Society of Physiotherapy, offers a national credit-based programme for physiotherapists even though the University itself does not provide physiotherapy training. Indeed, it was its neutrality in this respect, and its expertise in managing credit, that made it the preferred partner. A similar partnership with a London-based consortium of social workers was established on the same principle. In this way, universities and colleges might seek to sell their expertise rather than their provision.

National Council for Vocational Qualifications

In parallel with all these developments, however, the relationship between education and the workplace has increasingly been dominated by the emergence of the National Council for Vocational Qualifications (NCVQ). It is a subject that warrants (and will undoubtedly receive) the attention of a full book. It is a body that from the very beginning has troubled almost all of higher education. The higher education jury would still probably have a majority decision of guilty, but increasingly there is at least a pragmatic view that the Council is unlikely to go away, and the best response to it is to find ways of working with it.

There is a long tradition among CAT practitioners of antagonism towards NCVQ. Part of the problem lies in the philosophical and ideological underpinnings of the concept of competence. To many, the fact that this approach was rejected in the US nearly three decades ago was sufficiently suggestive of its limitations. More practically, the NCVQ framework presented itself as *the* national credit framework, but was clearly not related conceptually or organizationally to *the* national framework which had been introduced by the CNAA or, for that matter *the* national credit framework set up by the Open College Network and later the FEU. It would also not be totally unfair to say that credit practitioners were no different from anyone else in preferring their own fundamental changes to those of others.

Articulation

As often happens, the various political agendas have turned the debate around. The NCVQ made it clear it was here to stay, and the government made it equally clear that it would support it. The last nail in the coffin, probably, was the announcement that NVQs would be tax-deductible. But NCVQ started, particularly as it moved to Levels 4 and 5, to publicly acknowledge the existence and significance of knowledge and understanding as central to training and education. Meanwhile, educationalists sought to retain distance, while accepting reality, by looking at the way the different credit frameworks could be 'articulated'. Like out-of-court settlements, this in no way admitted guilt or responsibility on either side, but allowed things to move on without too many unsightly squabbles. As usually happens, some staff – and here the

Business Schools were the first in – found a market, developed techniques and eventually set up their own awarding body, the Management Verification Consortium (MVC).

It would be untrue to say that higher education has taken NCVQ to its heart, but the mood has undoubtedly changed in those areas where NVQs are either a reality or near at hand. The introduction of the GNVQ, a creature that bears at least some similarity to conventional provision offered by further and higher education and which accepts that educational institutions might actually be useful, was initially greeted with somewhat more warmth. This, it was thought, could be the Trojan horse into the system, though it is still unclear whether the occupants are from the Employment Department or from the universities and colleges. Despite some stern, if not always well-founded, criticism, the take-off of the Advanced GNVQ, even if just in terms of sheer numbers, further establishes NCVQ on the higher education landscape.

The issue now for credit practitioners is how to relate the two systems. Much exploratory work is being done, procedures developed, good practice determined. For example, the portfolio which has been used by many for determining APL within the CNAA credit framework is a portable tool that can be used for NVQs. Additionally, it is evident that individuals with NVQs often wish to have appropriate higher education credits attached, so that they can move on to recognized higher education awards. Much of the work that has gone on over the years in the area of external credit-rating becomes a useful and customizable tool. Once again, when barriers start to fall, or are broken down, credit proves itself a flexible tool for smoothing change.

Interested parties

It is also the case that the Employment Department has been keen to support general developments in the area of credit, while emphasizing its commitment to NVQs. At the Learning Without Walls conference in 1991, the Department's submission stated that:

> *CAT may be seen both as a form of quality assurance and as a means of offering certificated learning in achievable amounts. Valid certification is itself a motivator of individual investment.*

Training and Enterprise Councils, the major vehicle for implementing NVQs, have also begun to show an interest in wider developments in credit. Most notably, in 1993, the Chief Executives of the coordinated London TECs made a statement calling for the adoption of a CAT Manifesto. Their statement was unusually clear in saying:

> *Credit Accumulation and Transfer is an idea whose time has come...TECs have an important role to play, both in progressing CAT more quickly than might otherwise be the case, and in setting the CAT agenda which might otherwise be dominated by concerns that have a lower priority for TECs.*

This subsequently led to a partnership with London Together, a further and higher education credit consortium; a successful bid for £250,000 from the Single Regeneration Budget; and the establishment in 1995 of a London CAT Consortium.

When combined with a £200,000 Employment Department project, managed by the South East England Consortium (SEEC), to determine the feasibility of a regional credit agency, it becomes apparent that the support for credit has moved well beyond institutional boundaries and the education institutions themselves.

Conclusion

The use of credit to incorporate 'off-campus' learning will continue to expand, involving a wider range of organizations, and will be used to install a new set of relationships with employers and employees. This chapter has, however, looked at the way in which such developments have, in addition, considerable symbolic and political significance that is disproportionate either to their ability to generate income or to deliver student numbers. In particular, they identify the ability of institutions to move beyond their walls; they demonstrate the principle that learning can take place anywhere; they provide a safe, and limited, environment in which to develop precedent and practice; and they can provide a high profile baseline from which broader developments in credit and unitization can take place. In the history of the development of credit-based systems, their impact will be seen to be small in quantitative, but large in qualitative, terms.

Postscript

In the final chapter of his report on the future of credit-based systems, *Choosing to Change*, David Robertson ambitiously took on the question of how within the UK it could be possible to develop what he calls 'a credit culture'. To him credit-based systems are an element of a scenario in which 'universities and colleges are being transformed from sheltered institutions of the pre-modern world to public service organisations in a modern (or some would suggest, post-modern) world' (1994, p.313). For him the alternatives for the development of credit-based systems are stark. Are credit systems to be little more than administrative devices which will provide limited flexibility and choice for students, but have little impact on the basic nature of academic institutions? Or do we require fundamental change which would involve an intellectual reconfiguration of institutional practice, with profound consequences including, in Robertson's view, a shift in the taxonomies of knowledge, the rewriting of the undergraduate curriculum, the evolution of the academic profession, and the fundamental reconstruction of the institution? These changes would lead, he says to:

> *the creation of a new balance of power between managers and academic faculty, the erosion of traditional demarcations between higher and other forms of post-secondary education, the blurring of disciplinary boundaries and the deconstruction of absolute forms of professional control over the curriculum and its meaning for students.* (p.316)

The report, which backs up this radical rhetoric with 104 detailed recommended actions for a range of stakeholders, has predictably been greeted with a variety of responses ranging from eulogy to outrage to indifference. This will not have been surprising either to the report's author, those of us who were involved in its production, or its readers. Indeed, many of us have welcomed the controversy and debate.

If credit is to be a major tool by which institutions will organize their academic delivery, its introduction and implementation requires that there be a proper understanding of the political and philosophical sources; the context in which it has come about; the patterns, processes and practices of its delivery; and the implications for staff and students. For such a major educational change, the literature has so far been curiously lacking but Robertson has filled much of that gap. More significantly, it is a report that, unlike much other literature in this field, is being read by principal stakeholders within government, the professions and the funding councils, as well as by senior managers within institutions. Whether they will like it, accept it or act upon it remains to be seen. But in any case, it is probably not the major purpose which such a report can serve.

Within the model of effective management proposed by Eccles and Nohria, which was introduced in Chapter 1, and which focused around rhetoric, action and identity, the broader value of the Robertson Report might be seen more clearly. It sets out, in a very powerful way, the language within which the debate about future change will take place. In its rehearsal of history, debate and practice it can act as the focus for the rhetoric that actors within the component elements of the higher education system must use. This does not mean, however, that it has been taken on board *in toto*. It is for the various players, whether they be within institutions, agencies or government departments, to determine how to act. The report's recommendations may be desirable, feasible, appropriate, but their significance lies in the fact that they become part of that rhetoric rather than that they must provide specific solutions.

If the report is so powerful, then it might be a matter of some regret that it was not produced earlier. Could it have provided the biblical text that practitioners have sought over the years? The answer of course is that it could not. The report might have been written at any stage over the last 15 years and, indeed, some others were. But this report is constructed from earlier rhetoric and, more importantly, subsequent actions. It reflects in this way the complex and dynamic relationship between language and action. Action not only comes out of language, it is the means by which language is constructed and reconstructed. When setting out to write this book, for example, we were very keen not to use the term CAT unless it represented either historical practice or a specific individual perspective. The term lay for us in the past, useful at the time, but no longer serving a helpful purpose. It had allowed us to act in the early days, but now no longer represented what we were trying to do, and increasingly had become a barrier to change.

It is interesting that one of the criticisms of the Robertson Report is that it is too academic. Given that one of the premises of the report is that a major barrier to the development of a credit culture is academic resistance, what better language to use therefore than that of the very people who most need to read it. And, indeed, comments from academic colleagues about the Robertson Report often go along the lines that it is a very good and stimulating read, but that they disagree with a lot of it. For the credit practitioner, that is progress indeed!

The Robertson Report has come out at a point in time when there is probably a watershed in the development of credit-based systems in the UK. Many institutions have committed themselves to developing modular schemes; most have attached themselves to the CNAA's credit tariff. While many observers would argue that much of this change is little more than cosmetic, it means that they have accepted the possibility that it could be a useful tool in facilitating future change. The fact that the actions resulting from the use of the language of credit are highly variable between institutions, and quite limited in the case of a substantial minority, does not undermine its significance. Many institutions see the potential need for the use of credit-based systems. In this sense they accept its rhetoric. But the actions they take will be based on the specific history, needs and mission reflecting both the institution's identity and that of its managers and staff. Credit-based systems are now prevalent enough for us to be able to see how some institutions have carried their actions through on the back of that rhetoric. It remains to be seen how, and in what ways, others choose to carry it forward.

The importance of the Robertson Report may therefore better be understood in five years' time. But meanwhile it reflects the fact that while there have been significant developments, credit-based systems do not yet, and may never, constitute the fundamental tool for change that some claim. Meanwhile, within institutions, the day-to-day business of introducing credit-based systems continues. It has been principally this level of action on which this book has concentrated. The wider debates which are rehearsed within both this book and the Robertson Report will provide a resonance for most credit practitioners. They will see themselves and their colleagues (in their various guises) in elements of both. They will empathize with the values and grandeur of the exercise undertaken by the report. They will not, of course, find out what to do. Nor will they find answers by reading this book. In looking at the management of change from an individual perspective, we have reinforced the view that the introduction of credit-based systems is institutionally and personally unique. Though many issues may be common, the actions required to resolve them within any one institutional context will vary dramatically. There may be models, but they are only that. There may be good practice, but it may not be appropriate or feasible for a particular situation. What there certainly isn't, is the grand design. Pilgrimages may make you feel good and provide you with some vision. They may even tell you or your institution the best way to lead your life. But they will not resolve the issue of how through the institutional tools available – the people, structures, documents, committees – it is possible to introduce appropriate credit-based schemes. Nor will the management gurus provide the answers. As Eccles and Nohria conclude, they cannot offer 'a pithy concluding statement regarding "what you should do next" '. In the end, they say, managers must adapt words and concepts to their own circumstances (1992, p.205).

Those words would therefore be the message, if such it has, of this book. But we would also stress the final component of Eccles and Nohria's formula: identity. If credit practitioners have had a major failure, it has been their understandable overemphasis on the student experience. It is clear from the experience of many institutions that this worthy goal cannot be achieved without taking account of the experience of staff – academic and administrative – in the change process. The ability to bring a sufficient number of staff along with the purposes of credit-based systems, and to ensure that within the new structures they can construct an adequate and satisfying identity as teacher and researcher, is the major problem. In the end it is the relationship of the language and actions of credit-based systems to the experience and identity of staff that will ensure the successful implementation of credit-based systems.

References

Alderman, G (1995) *A Degree of Association, Guardian*, 11 April 1995.

Allen, R (1988) *Development of Credit Accumulation and Transfer in Non-Modular Schemes: An Overview*, London: University of Greenwich.

CIHE (1987) *Towards a Partnership: Higher Education–Government–Industry*, London: CIHE.

Davidson, G (1992) 'Credit Accumulation and Transfer and the Student Experience' in R Barnett (ed.) *Learning to Effect*, Buckingham: SRHE/Open University.

Eccles, R and Nohria, N (1992) *Beyond the Hype*, Boston: Harvard College.

Evans, N (1988) *The Assessment of Prior Experiential Learning*, London: CNAA.

Hilton, A and Ellis, D (eds) (1991) *Learning Without Walls*, Oxford: SEEC.

Kanter, R M (1983) *The Change Masters*, New York: Simon and Schuster.

Middlehurst, R (1993) *Leading Academics*, Buckingham: SRHE/Open University.

Mintzberg, H (1983) *Power in and Around Organizations*, New Jersey: Prentice-Hall.

Peters, T (1992) *Liberation Management*, New York: Alfred Knopf.

Price, C (1994) 'Piloting Higher Education Change: A View from the Helm' in S Weil (ed.) *Managing Change from the Top in Universities and Colleges*, London: Kogan Page.

Regel, O (1992) *The Academic Credit System in Higher Education: Effectiveness and Relevance in Developing Countries*, Washington: World Bank.

Robbins, Lord (1963) *Report of the Committee on Higher Education*, London: HMSO.

Robertson, D (1994) *Choosing to Change: Extending Access, Choice and Mobility in Higher Education*, London: HEQC.

Stoddart, J (1990) *Developments in Continuing Education: The Next Ten Years*, Nottingham: PACE/Employment Department.

Theodossin, E (1986) *The Modular Market*, Bristol: Further Education Staff College.

Toyne, P (1979) *Educational Credit Transfer: A Feasibility Study*, London: DES.

Watson, D (1989) *Managing the Modular Course*, Buckingham: SRHE/Open University.

Webb, A (1994) 'Two Tales from a Reluctant Manager', in S Weil (ed.) *Managing Change from the Top in Universities and Colleges*, London: Kogan Page.

Weil, S (ed.) (1994) *Managing Change from the Top in Universities and Colleges*, London: Kogan Page.

Glossary of Abbreviations

AAU	Academic Audit Unit
APEL	assessment of prior experiential learning
APL	assessment of prior learning
BTEC	Business and Technician Education Council
CAT	Credit Accumulation and Transfer
CBI	Confederation of British Industry
CNAA	Council for National Academic Awards
CPD	Continuing Professional Development
CVCP	Committee of Vice-Chancellors and Principals
DfE	Department for Education
ECCTIS	Educational Counselling and Credit Transfer Information Service
EFTA	European Free Trade Association
EHE	Enterprise in Higher Education
EU	European Union
FEU	Further Education Unit
GCSE	General Certificate in Secondary Education
GNVQ	General National Vocational Qualification
HEFC	Higher Education Funding Council
HEQC	Higher Education Quality Council
HMI	Her Majesty's Inspectorate
HND	Higher National Diploma
ICS	Integrated Credit Scheme
IiP	Investor in People
INSET	In-service Training
MSC	Manpower Services Commission
MUGS	Modular Users Group, South
MVC	Management Verification Consortium
NATFHE	National Association of Teachers in Further and Higher Education
NCVQ	National Council for Vocational Qualifications
NVQ	National Vocational Qualification
NZQA	New Zealand Qualifications Authority
OCN	Open College Network
OU	Open University
PACE	Polytechnic Association for Continuing Education
SEEC	South East England Consortium
SNVQ	Scottish National Vocational Qualification
SRHE	Society for Research into Higher Education
TEC	Training and Enterprise Council

Index